new and expanded edition

poetry like bread

Poets of the Political Imagination from Curbstone Press

Edited by Martín Espada

C U R B S T O N E   P R E S S

New and expanded edition: 2000
The first edition was published in 1994, reprinted in 1996 and 1998.

Printed on acid-free paper by Best Book / Transcon Printing
cover design: Les Kanturek

All of the poems in this collection, except for Rigoberta Menchú's poem, are from poetry books that Curbstone Press has published or has contracted to publish. We gratefully thank all of these outstanding writers for contributing their poems to this collection.

Rigoberta Menchú's poem "Patria abnegada" appears by the permission of the Vicente Menchú Foundation, a human rights organization dedicated to seeking out and developing projects that support the rights of indigenous peoples of Guatemala and elsewhere, and educating policy makers and the general public on issues surrounding human rights and peace.

This book, like many of the books represented here, was published with support from the Connecticut Commission on the Arts, the National Endowment for the Arts, and donations from many individuals. We are very grateful for this support.

Library of Congress Cataloging-in-Publication Data

    Poetry like bread : poets of the political imagination from Curbstone
    Press / edited by Martín Espada. — New and expanded.
      p. cm.
    ISBN 1-880684-74-8
      1. Political poetry. I. Espada, Martín, 1957-
    PN6110.P728 P64 2000
    808.81'9358'09045—dc21   00-060358

published by
CURBSTONE PRESS
321 Jackson Street, Willimantic, CT 06226

PN6110
.P728
P64
2000

Praise for the first edition of *Poetry like Bread*

"Espada's collection will remain as a testament to the artistry and commitment of some of the most powerful poets of the Americas."—Brian Henry, *Richmond Times Dispatch*

"A unique anthology..."—*Booklist*

"Strength and integrity...unify these writers as they speak passionately on issues common to all countries."
—*Publishers Weekly*

"These are poems not so much of witness and survival as of defiance and resistance. That they all came from one small press alone suggests the plenitude of late Twentieth Century political poetry."—*The Progressive*

"The poems here are full of surprises, grand themes grounded in the painful and triumphant particulars of each poet's life."
—*National Catholic Reporter*

"*Poetry Like Bread* is an engrossing, readable, and highly passionate poetry anthology....It gives us poetry that sustains, that nourishes, and that is available to all. This is a book that gives me hope for the future of American poetry."—*Poetry Flash*

"...The one volume of overtly political poetry, though, that I would most like to wave from the ramparts... These works demonstrate with eloquence that the task of poetry—and all literature—is to challenge us, to illuminate our world and our lives, to force us to examine that which we take for granted and to act in solidarity for something new, to 'give name to the nameless so it can be thought.'"—Chris Faatz, *The Nation*

"For its inclusiveness and imagination, *Poetry Like Bread* is a collection to be celebrated."—Jeanne E. Clark, *Bilingual Review*

"This beautifully edited anthology of urgent and necessary poetry... is one of the few collections of poetry that reflects suffering and resistance, as well as the bravery and love that motivate all people who seek a better and more just world. These poems provide the inspiration to carry on this struggle in hostile times. In its political character, *Poetry Like Bread* is unique; for the richness of the work it contains, it is essential."—Carolyn Forché

Contents

POETRY LIKE BREAD

ON *POETRY LIKE BREAD*

The feelings of the poets in this book—the sensitivity, tenderness, rebelliousness and patience that point to the future for our América—confront the moral crisis and desperation we witness in the gross materialism permeating our societies. With bold and simple words, they speak to us of the women and men who build hope every day. So we are able to perceive the courage and suffering of those who are, in the final analysis,

> the silenced majority
> that some day
> will decide
> which small piece of the sky
> belongs to them.

> —Rigoberta Menchú
> 1992 Nobel Peace Prize

Patria abnegada

Crucé la frontera amor,
no sé cuando volveré.
Tal vez cuando sea verano,
cuando abuelita luna y padre sol
se saluden otra vez,
en una madrugada esclareciente,
festejados por todas las estrellas,
anunciarán las primeras lluvias,
retoñarán los ayotes que sembró Víctor
en esa tarde que fue fusilado pos militares,
florecerán los duraznales,
florecerán nuestros campos.
Sembraremos mucho maíz.
Maíz para todas los hijos de nuestra tierra.
Regresarán los enjambres de abejas que huyeron
por tantas masacres y tanto terror.
Saldrán de nuevo de las manos callosas tinajas
y más tinajas para cosechar la miel.

Crucé la frontera empapada de tristeza.
Siento inmenso dolor de esa madrugada
lluviosa y oscura,
que va más allá de mi existencia.
Lloran los mapaches, lloran los saraguates,
los coyotes y sensontles totalmente silenciosos,
los caracoles y los jutes desean hablar.
La tierra madre está de luto, empañada de sangre.
Llora día y noche de tanta tristeza.
Le faltarán los arrullos de los azadones,
los arrullos de los machetes,
los arrullos de las piedras de moler.
En cada amanecer estará ansiosa de escuchar
risas y cantos de sus gloriosos hijos.

My Martyred Homeland

I crossed the border, my love,
I do not know when I will return.
Maybe in summer
when grandmother moon and father sun
greet one another again,
on the illuminated early morning
celebrated by every star,
heralding the first rains;
the pumpkins Víctor sowed that afternoon
the soldiers shot him will sprout again,
the peach orchards will bloom,
our fields will bloom.
We will plant an abundance of corn.
Corn for all the sons and daughters of our land.
The swarms of bees will return
that fled from so many massacres, so much terror.
Jar after earthenware jar will come again
from callused hands for harvesting the honey.

I crossed the border drenched in sadness.
I feel immense grief on this early morning,
rainy, dark,
so much greater than my existence.
The raccoons cry, the howler monkeys cry,
the coyotes and mockingbirds are totally silent,
the sea-snails and river-snails want to speak.
Mother Earth is dressed in mourning, swaddled in blood.
She cries day and night in such sorrow.
She will miss the lullaby of pickaxes,
the lullaby of machetes,
the lullaby of grinding-stones.
With every daybreak she will strain to hear
the laughing and singing of her exalted children.

Crucé la frontera cargada de dignidad.
Llevo el costal lleno de tantas cosas
de esa tierra lluviosa.
Llevo los recuerdos milenarios de Patrocinio,
los caites que nacieron conmigo,
el olor de la primavera,
olor de los musgos, las caricias de la milpa
y los gloriosos callos de la infancia.
Llevo el huipil colorial
para la fiesta cuando regrese.
Llevo los huesos y el resto de maíz. ¡Pues sí!
Este costal volverá a donde salió,
pase lo que pase.

Crucé la frontera amor.
Volveré mañana, cuando mamá torturada
teja otro huipil multicolor,
cuando papá quemado vivo madrugue otra vez,
para saludar el sol desde las cuatro esquinas
de nuestro ranchito.
Entonces habrá cuxa para todos, habrá Pom,
la risa de los patojos, habrán marimbas alegres.
Habrán lumbres en cada ranchito, en cada río
para lavar el Nixtamal en la madrugada.
Se encenderán los ocotes, alumbrarán las veredas,
las rocas, los barrancos, y los campos.

—Rigoberta Menchú T.
enero de 1991, Li Miin

I crossed the border burdened with dignity.
I carry a sack loaded with many things
from that rainswept land.
I carry the ancient memories of Patrocinio,
the sandals born with me,
smell of spring,
smell of moss, caress of the cornfield,
and the blessed calluses of childhood.
I carry my bright huipil
for the fiesta of my return.
I carry the bones and the last of the corn. Well, yes!
Whatever happens,
this sack will return
to the place it left behind.

I crossed the border, my love.
I will return tomorrow, when my tortured mother
weaves another huipil of many colors,
when my father burned alive rises early once more
to greet the sun from the four corners
of our small farmhouse.
Then there will be homemade rum for everyone, incense,
the laughter of children, jubilant marimbas.
There will be fires lit at every farmhouse, at every river
to wash the corn for tortillas in the early morning.
We will burn torches of pine to light the footpaths,
the rocks, the cliffs, and the fields.

> —Rigoberta Menchú T.
> January 1991, Li Miin
> *translated by Martín Espada & Camilo Pérez-Bustillo*

FOREWORD

In his landmark essay, "In Defense of the Word," Eduardo Galeano writes: "We are what we do, especially what we do to change what we are...A literature born in the process of crisis and change, and deeply immersed in the risks and events of its time, can indeed help to create the symbols of the new reality, and perhaps—if talent and courage are not lacking—throw light on the signs along the road...To claim that literature on its own is going to change reality would be an act of madness or arrogance. It seems to me no less foolish to deny that it can aid in making this change." This anthology is founded on such convictions.

This is, first of all, a Curbstone Press anthology. All of the poets presented here have books published or forthcoming with Curbstone. This anthology is a document of Curbstone's history as a visionary, politically progressive publisher, a tribute to the work of its co-editors, Alexander Taylor and Judith Ayer Doyle. Curbstone was publishing Central American authors in translation during the mid-1970s, at a time when most people in this country thought "Central America" meant Ohio. In recent years, Curbstone has expanded its vision to include the work of significant U.S. Latino writers. For a quarter of a century, the press has been a catalyst at the core of the literary left in the United States, which does indeed exist and organizes itself around such publishers as Curbstone.

This is also a truly "American" anthology, not in the conventional sense of the United States alone, but in the sense of "América" with an accent. Poets from New York, yes, but also Tegucigalpa. This meeting of North and South is unusual among poetry anthologies. Here we find a striking commonality of purpose and tactic, a solidarity born of the fact that one's own quiet labor in the dark is the shadow of the same act committed by others in the same clandestine dark thousands of miles away.

Poetry of the political imagination is a matter of both vision and language. Any progressive social change must be imagined first, and that vision must find its most eloquent possible expression to move from vision to reality. Any oppressive social condition, before it can change, must be named and condemned in words that persuade by stirring the emotions, awakening the senses. Thus the need for the political imagination.

Political imagination goes beyond protest to articulate an *artistry* of dissent. The question is not whether poetry and politics can mix. That question is a luxury for those who can afford it. The question is how *best* to combine poetry and politics, craft and commitment, how to find the artistic imagination equal to the intensity of the experience and the quality of the ideas.

There is a great poetic tradition of the political imagination in the Americas, embodied by Walt Whitman in the North and Pablo Neruda in the South. In his 1855 introduction to *Leaves of Grass,* Whitman indicates that the duty of the poet is "to cheer up slaves and horrify despots." In Neruda we encounter Whitman's most eloquent descendant. Radicalized by the Spanish Civil War, he articulates his metamorphosis in "I Explain a Few Things": "You will ask: why does your poetry / not speak to us of sleep, of the leaves, / of the great volcanoes of your native land? / Come and see the blood in the streets, / come and see / the blood in the streets, / come and see the blood / in the streets!"

The language produced by this political imagination is often clear, concrete, urgently direct. Though sometimes written to be read aloud, these are not campaign speeches. The appeal to the senses, the image, is still there: what better way to describe the haze in a polluted sky than Jack Hirschman's "tortillas of smog"? Indeed, poets of the political imagination often have the art of metaphor, of finding the face which is many faces, of finding the moment which stands for a century. Ernesto Cardenal's captured—and liberated—parrots become rebellious guerrillas in Nicaragua; Roque Dalton's torture victim looks up at the "perfect" glass eye of his torturer, made in the United States, and sees the physical manifestation of U.S. foreign policy in El Salvador.

Though some political works are solely works of the imagination, many, if not most, are drawn directly from lived experience, contradicting a certain critical notion that political poems are written after a morning reading the newspaper, as the poet searches for a headline which will be sufficiently infuriating to inspire a burst of rhetoric. Many, if not most, political poets are personally familiar with the rhythms of oppression. The reader only has to encounter the startling prison poems of Jimmy Santiago Baca to appreciate that particular music. A social horror is focused through the prism of the poet's understanding, and the reader unfamiliar with the experience finds his or her own imagination engaged and politicized. Or the experience may prove surprisingly familiar: virtually anyone who reads Baca's "I Applied for the Board," about the denial of parole, can identify with the trajectory of anticipation and disappointment sketched in the poem.

More than mere victims, however, the poets of these pages are activists, political participants. Jack Hirschman and Sara Menefee fight for the rights of the homeless in San Francisco. Kevin Bowen is the head of an agency which serves Vietnam veterans and works towards a reconciliation with Vietnam. Luis Rodríguez works with peacemakers among gangs in Los Angeles and elsewhere. Víctor Montejo, from exile, speaks out publicly against the suffering of his own Mayan people in Guatemala. Several of the poets in this volume have engaged in the deeply political act of armed insurrection: Roque Dalton, Otto René Castillo, Leonel Rugama, and Daisy Zamora.

Three of these four poets—Dalton, Castillo and Rugama—were murdered for political reasons; most grotesquely of all, Castillo was burned alive by the Guatemalan military in 1967. Many of the poets in this anthology (including Dalton, Castillo, Montejo, Hirschman, Menefee, Rodríguez, James Scully, and Clemente Soto Vélez) have been jailed for political reasons, some for days, others for many years. Still more have been forced into political exile, such as Ernesto Cardenal, Claribel Alegría, Gioconda Belli, Paul Laraque, and Alfonso Quijada Urías. Some have suffered unique forms of political persecution, as with the U.S. government's attempts to deport Margaret Randall.

Not surprisingly, resistance is a major theme of the political in this book. The poets are careful to insist upon the kind of intimate details that give politics a human face. Thus Jimmy Santiago Baca reports to us, from the midst of a prison rebellion, of men singing, "in the smoke and bars in their cells, they sing!" As a combatant in the Sandinista revolution, Daisy Zamora vividly recalls a friend making his way across a battlefield through "sporadic bursts of gunfire," as she and others watched, "our hearts beating uselessly." While some poets speak openly of political insurgency, others focus on the personal revolution of thought and language, which in turn become liberating forces. So

Clemente Soto Vélez, a Puerto Rican independentista imprisoned for seditious conspiracy, writes of "the thinking peon," the "peon of the subversive verb." As this vocabulary makes clear, the poets rightly regard their verbs as subversive, each poem as a political act in itself.

The same poets are committed advocates, speaking for the voices struck silent, living or dead. The poets tell us of being haunted by this song of the voiceless. In "Nocturnal Visits," Alegría speaks of "the amputated / the cripples / those who lost both legs / both eyes / the stammering teenagers. / At night I listen to their phantoms / shouting in my ear." In "Then Comes a Day," Luis Rodríguez visits a barrio cemetery filled with his dead friends and writes: "I have carried the obligation to these names. / I have honored their voices / still reverberating through me." Gioconda Belli remembers Nicaragua's dead in "The Blood of Others" and "In Memoriam." Indeed, these are poets who pay tribute to their dead, so many dead, from the internationally known, such as Víctor Jara, the singer and guitarist slain by the military in the Chilean coup, to the anonymous, who would dissolve into oblivion without the poets.

Both Whitman and Neruda expressly embraced the role of the poet as advocate, and in so doing influenced generations of poets. Whitman, in #24 of "Song of Myself," proclaims: "through me many long dumb voices, / voices of the interminable generations of prisoners and slaves, / voices of the diseas'd and despairing and of thieves and dwarfs...voices veiled and I remove the veil." Neruda, standing at the Heights of Macchu Picchu, speaking to centuries of dead laborers, says in Canto 12: "Look at me from the depths of the earth, / tiller of fields, weaver, reticent shepherd...jeweler with crushed fingers, / farmer anxious among his seedlings, / potter wasted among his clays...I come to speak for your dead mouths." The poet's advocacy springs from compassion, and compassion is the poet's pulse. Whitman again: "whoever walks a furlong without sympathy walks to / his own funeral drest in his shroud."

The poems document daily existence as well, finding the political in the everyday. There is, for example, invaluable documentation of working-class lives, and the struggle to transcend dehumanizing labor. Leo Connellan movingly writes of Amelia, a woman of the canneries in Maine. Kevin Bowen brings us the "Gelatin Factory," and Luis

Rodríguez "The Blast Furnace." Cheryl Savageau tells of dangerous work with silicon, pesticides and asbestos. There is unemployment too, as in Savageau's "Department of Labor Haiku": "In the winter snow / the kitchens fill up with steam / and men out of work." If the workplace is political, then so too is the home, with its cycles of violence evoked in a few brushstrokes by Leroy Quintana's "Poem for U-Haul:" "The highway was made / for a morning like this. / A woman with two sad blackeyes. Never / again, never, never again. Last night / was the last time, the last time, the last."

They also document the presence of such social forces as racism, sexism and poverty, and in so doing make those abstract terms painfully concrete. Tino Villanueva constructs the personification of anti-Mexican bigotry in his portrayal of Sarge, a character from the movie *Giant* who enforces, with his "thick arms," the rules of segregation in a Texas diner. The major Puerto Rican poet Julia de Burgos, before her early death in 1953, anticipated the rise of feminism with "To Julia de Burgos," a condemnation of suffocating social convention: "who governs in me is me." Her literary descendant, Naomi Ayala of Puerto Rico, writes that "poverty is black ice," and so captures the precarious sensation of being poor.

The poems in this collection not only condemn, but appreciate. Claribel Alegría appreciates Carmen Bomba, "porter...human beast of burden" and "poet." Jimmy Santiago Baca, as one who has known brutal incarceration, can proclaim "Ah Rain!" and mean it, passionately, politically. Jack Hirschman pauses at a political rally to observe a butterfly walking across a newspaper in "This Neruda Earth." There is even an appreciation for the absurd, as in the satirical Doug Anderson poem, "Town Meeting," depicting a debate on the homeless in a college town.

In fact, perhaps the most remarkable characteristic found in the poetry of the political imagination is the quality of hopefulness, testimony to the extraordinary resilience of that human quality. The prophetic voice resonates throughout the poetry; the poets sing of the possibility, the *certainty* of eventual justice. Alegría, a poet "condemned so many times / to be a crow," is able to fly, "and amid valleys / volcanoes / and debris of war / I catch sight of the promised land." Soto Vélez, also a poet of the "promised land," predicts that "the hands / of the peon" will "thunder in the cartilage of the future." Alfonso Quijada Urías of El Salvador envisions a time when the grocer will use the poet's writings as paper funnels "to wrap up his sugar and coffee / for the people of the future / who now for obvious reasons / cannot savor his sugar nor his coffee." Most poignantly, the murdered Castillo writes that it is "splendid / to know yourself victorious / when all around you / it's all still so cold, / so dark."

This is the height of political imagination, in the sense of the poet as visionary, again echoing Neruda and Whitman. Neruda could peer back into history and foresee contemporary resistance movements in México and Perú with his poems for Emiliano Zapata and Tupac Amarú—movements, in fact, which would adopt the very names of these revolutionaries. Whitman could gaze upon the slave at auction and see "the father of those who shall be fathers in their turns, / In him the start of populous states and rich republics, / Of him countless immortal lives with countless embodiments and enjoyments."

What else but defiant, extravagant hope—political imagination— could motivate Roque Dalton, a man who suffered imprisonment and ultimately assassination, to write the words that give this anthology its title: "I believe the world is beautiful / and that poetry, like bread, is for everyone."

Martín Espada

poetry
like
bread

Ars Poética

Yo,
poeta de oficio,
condenada tantas veces
a ser cuervo
jamás me cambiaría
por la Venus de Milo:
mientras reina en el Louvre
y se muere de tedio
y junta polvo
yo descubro el sol
todos los días
y entre valles
volcanes
y despojos de guerra
avizoro la tierra prometida.

Ars Poetica

I,
poet by trade,
condemned so many times
to be a crow,
would never change places
with the Venus de Milo:
while she reigns in the Louvre
and dies of boredom
and collects dust
I discover the sun
each morning
and amid valleys
volcanoes
and debris of war
I catch sight of the promised land.

translated by Darwin J. Flakoll

Visitas Nocturnas

Pienso en nuestros anónimos muchachos
en nuestros héroes apagados
los mancos
los rencos
los que perdieron las dos piernas
los dos ojos
los casi niños balbucientes.
Escucho por las noches sus fantasmas
gritándome al oído
me sacan del letargo
me conminan
pienso en su vida hecha girones
en sus febriles manos
queriendo asir las nuestras.
No es que estén mendigando
nos exigen
se han ganado el derecho a exigir
a romper nuestro sueño
a despertarnos
a sacudir de una vez
esta modorra.

Nocturnal Visits

I think of our anonymous boys
of our burnt-out heroes
the amputated
the cripples
those who lost both legs
both eyes
the stammering teen-agers.
At night I listen to their phantoms
shouting in my ear
shaking me out of lethargy
issuing me commands
I think of their tattered lives
of their feverish hands
reaching out to seize ours.
It's not that they're begging
they're demanding
they've earned the right to order us
to break up our sleep
to come awake
to shake off once and for all
this lassitude.

translated by Darwin J. Flakoll

Los Ríos

Es abrupto el terreno
en mi país
se le secan los cauces
en verano y se tiñen de rojo
en el invierno.
Hierve el Sumpul de muertos
decía aquella madre
el Goascorán
el Lempa
todos hierven de muertos.
Ya no cantan los ríos
se lamentan
arrastran a sus muertos
los arrullan
bajo la luna tibia
parpadean
bajo la noche cómplice
y oscura
arrullan a sus muertos
al herido
a los que andan huyendo
a los que pasan
se ponen iracundos
borbotean
el alba ya está cerca
ya se toca
son ataúd los ríos
probetas de cristal
arrullan a sus muertos
los custodian

The Rivers

The terrain in my country
is abrupt
the gullies go dry
in the summertime
and are stained with red
in the winter.
The Sumpul is boiling with corpses
a mother said
the Goascarán
the Lempa
are all boiling with the dead.
The rivers no longer sing
they lament
they sweep their dead along
cradle them
they twinkle
under the tepid moon
under the dark
accomplice night
they cradle their dead
the wounded
those who are fleeing
those who pass by
they grow irate
bubbling and seething
dawn draws near
almost within reach
the rivers are coffins
crystalline flasks
cradling their dead
escorting them

entre sus anchas márgenes
navegan
y los recoge el mar
y resucitan.

between their wide banks
the dead sail down
and the sea receives them
and they revive.

translated by Darwin J. Flakoll

Carmen Bomba

A Luisa le refrescaba el recuerdo de Carmen Bomba, el cargador de muebles en el mercado de Santa Ana. Todas las tardes, después de su trabajo se emborrachaba un poquito para coger valor y se asomaba a las ventanas abiertas del vecindario a soltar las rimas que había compuesto ese día.

Carmen Bomba: Poet

Luisa always felt refreshed when she remembered Carmen Bomba, the porter and human beast of burden in the Santa Ana marketplace. Each afternoon when he finished work he'd get a bit drunk to arouse his courage, and he'd pause before each open window in the neighborhood to recite the verses he had composed that day.

translated by Darwin J. Flakoll

Desde el puente

He salido por fin
me ha costado salir
casi al final del puente
me detengo
el agua corre abajo
es un agua revuelta
arrastrando vestigios:
la voz de Carmen Lira
rostros que yo quería
y que pasaron.
Desde aquí
desde el puente
la perspectiva cambia
miro hacia atrás
hacia el comienzo:
la silueta indecisa
de una niña
de la mano le cuelga
una muñeca
la ha dejado caer
viene hacia mí la niña
ya es una adolescente
se recoge el cabello
y reconozco el gesto
detente ahí muchacha
si te acercas ahora
sería difícil conversar:
don Chico ya murió
después de siete operaciones
lo dejaron morir
en un pobre hospital
cerraron el colegio de Ricardo

From the Bridge

I have freed myself at last
it has been hard to break free
almost at the end of the bridge
I pause
the water flows below
a turbulent water
sweeping fragments with it:
the voice of Carmen Lira
faces that I loved
and I passed by.
From here
from the bridge
the perspective changes
I look backward
toward the beginning:
the hesitant silhouette
of a little girl
a doll
dangling from her hand
she lets it drop
and walks toward me
she is already adolescent
gathers up her hair
and I recognize the gesture
stop, girl
stop right there
if you come any closer
it will be difficult to talk:
Don Chico died
after seven operations
they let him die
in a charity hospital
they closed Ricardo's college

y él también murió
durante el terremoto
le falló el corazón.
¿Recuerdas la masacre
que dejó sin hombres
a Izalco?
Tenías siete años
¿cómo podré explicarte
que no ha cambiado nada
y que siguen matando diariamente?
Más vale que no sigas
te recuerdo bien a esa edad
escribías poemas almibarados
sentías horror por la violencia
enseñabas a leer
a los niños del barrio
¿qué dirías
si te contara que Pedro
tu mejor alumno
se pudrió en una cárcel
y que Sarita
la niña de ojos zarcos
que se inventaba cuentos
se dejó seducir
por el hijo mayor
de sus patrones
y después se vendía
por dos reales?
Has dado un paso más
llevas el pelo corto
y algunos textos
bajo el brazo
pobre ilusa
aprendiste la consolación
de la filosofía

and he died as well
during the earthquake
his heart failed.
Do you remember the massacre
that left Izalco without menfolk?
You were seven years old.
How can I explain it to you
nothing has changed
and they keep killing people daily.
It's better if you stop there
I remember you well at that age
you wrote honeyed poems
were horrified by violence
taught the neighborhood children
to read.
What would you say
if I told you that Pedro
your best student
rotted away in jail
and that Sarita
the little blue-eyed girl
who made up stories
let herself be seduced
by the eldest son
of her employers
and afterwards she sold herself
for twenty-five cents?
You've taken another step
you wear your hair short
have textbooks under your arm
poor deluded creature
you learned the consolations
of philosophy

antes de entender
de qué había que consolarse
tus libros te hablaban
de justicia
y cuidadosamente omitían
la inmundicia que nos rodea
desde siempre
tú seguías con tus versos
buscabas el orden en el caos
y ese fue tu norte
o quizá tu condena.
Te acercas más ahora
cuelgan niños de tus brazos
es fácil distraerse
con el papel de madre
y reducir el mundo
a un hogar.
Detente
no te acerques
aún no podrías reconocerme
aún tienes que pasar
por las muertes de Roque
de Rodolfo
por todas esas muertes
innumerables
que te asaltan
te acosan
te definen
para poder vestir este plumaje
(mi plumaje de luto)
para mirar
con estos ojos
despiadados
escrutadores
para tener mis garras
y este pico afilado.

before understanding
why you had to be consoled
your books spoke to you
of justice
and carefully omitted
the injustice
that has always surrounded us
you went on with your verses
searched for order in chaos
and that was your goal
or perhaps your condemnation.
You are coming closer now
your arms filled with children
it is easy to distract yourself
with a mother's role
and shrink the world
to a household.
Stop there
don't come any closer
you still wouldn't recognize me
you still have to undergo
the deaths of Roque
of Rodolfo
all those innumerable deaths
that assail you
pursue you
define you
in order to dress in these feathers
(my feathers of mourning)
to peer out
through these pitiless
scrutinizing eyes
to have my claws
and this sharp beak.

Nunca encontré el orden
que buscaba
siempre un desorden siniestro
y bien planificado
un desorden dosificado
que crece en manos
de los que ostentan el poder
mientras los otros
los que claman
por un mundo más cálido
con un menos de hambre
y un más de esperanza
mueren torturados
en la cárcel.
No te acerques más
hay un tufo a carroña
que me envuelve.

I never found the order
I searched for
but always a sinister
and well-planned disorder
that increases in the hands
of those who hold power
while the others
who clamor for
a more kindly world
a world with less hunger
and more hopefulness
die of torture
in the prisons.
Don't come any closer
there's a stench of carrion
surrounding me.

translated by Darwin J. Flakoll

Blues for Unemployed Mercenaries

For Martín Espada

The Hole, Rikers Island. Stainless steel toilet,
bunk, surveillance camera up in the shadows;
otherwise, the cell is empty. A powerfully built
man in early forties lit by soft glow sits on bunk.
Prison sounds in background. He speaks:

All I wanted was a goddam cab
and these two scumbags
had to say that thing about my hat,
I mean,
I was jet-lagged.
Hadn't been back from Joburg
two hours
these sorry fucks had to start:
Looka that hat. Whaddya work in a bathhouse?
Get me a towel, boy.
Then, heat-lightning,
snake-brain
to fingertips: I been trained.
Didn't even
take the time to love it,
my forty dollar hat
right down that guy's throat.
First thing here
got me another Turk hat
off a Muslim.
Word was out.
Nobody said nothin'
bout my hat. No
body. In the chow hall
guy looks at me

I say, You like my hat?
and he looks down.
Didn't say
I like your hat a whole lot
or
Your hat is positively chic
'cause he had a notion
I'd put my fork
through his adam's apple,
knew what to do;
not like these sorry fuck tourists,
reason I'm here.
Come through the trap
when I got here,
Chicom shrapnel in my ass
sets off the metal detector,
Guard says
I hear you like hats,
you wanna try to wear mine,
you fuck?
and they got me shackled
wrist to ankle
or I woulda rearranged
his chromosomes.
And then they strip search me
as if I'm dumb enough
to have contraband up my ass.
Went down to the yard,
parted the waters,
just walked through
and they stood aside
except for Mohammad
and his black ass is glad to see me
even if I am
an ice bullet man—'scuse me—
paramilitary consultant.

Fuckin' Afrikaners
never could get it right,
always too quick to load.
You don't take
the bullets out of the freezer
till the last,
keep some guys firing rubber bullets
till your snipers
can pick out the politicals
from their pictures,
then you load the ice
and drop the fuckers
and they haul them off to the morgue,
screaming,
I saw dem shoot, mon, I saw dem.
But when they cut 'em open
guess what melted
in all that blood and body heat.
Pick up my check and go to Bangkok,
shave my beard,
blend in with all the software salesmen
on a pussy hunt
and pretty soon I'm back in the world
except those sorry tourist fucks
had to say that about my hat
and now I'm in here.
I wish Yehuda would
get me out of here.
Don't care what I have to do
for him afterwards,
I mean, I'm a professional.
Worked for Pinochet.
I'll even work for NSA.
Anything but here.
Mother come by yesterday,
saw my picture in the paper.

Hadn't seen her for 10 years.
Sits down and starts to cry.
Says, I raised you Christian
and you come back from that war
meaner than a landlord.
I said Mama, in Pakistan
they take orphans and break
their legs
before they send them out to beg
and the people
who take their money at the end of the day
go home to fine houses.
That's the kind of world it is, Mama.
Yehuda's gonna get me out
and I'm gonna
take you to a French Restaurant,
show you what kind of money
an ice bullet man makes.
By the way, you like my hat?

The Torturer's Apprentice

Almost a man now,
he used to shudder
when the old man
slipped hatpin under fingernail
but now he's got
the master's calm,
the seducer's whiskey drift
to ply his subject
to give up his neighbor, tease
from him how many,
where and when.
Next month he'll have his first,
no more dabbing the old man's brow
with a cool towel,
no more sopping up the blood,
spraying air-freshener
to mask the lingering stink
of fear and anguish.
They've saved a little nun
for him, some dear thing
who still believes
that deep down people
are good.
We don't have to do this, Sister,
he'll say,
like a doctor, like a priest,
like he who giveth more
than you ever wanted.
Tell me
what I want to know
and I'll send you to God
with a single bullet in the nape.
You do not want
to finish this poem.

You do not want
to know who writes the check.
You do not want to know the fugitive self
you've sent down there,
where people do those things.
Where people do those things.

Colonial Album

For Yusef

They saw mirrored
in the gleaming teeth
everything they had always wanted
but were afraid to speak of,

lifted loincloths and peeked,
loved and beat the help alternately,
as required. There were parks
now on the islands where the vines

had been chastened and the trees
pruned. But inside the Masters,
the overgrowth burgeoned out
of control into endless expanses

of troubled dreams. You cannot
imagine their suffering (though
they lived long and were not sick),
nor their despair. Yet daguerreotypes
were made in which the Master
and his family were luminous
and impeccable with all
their brass buttons, the servants

shadows that broke off
like black lightning and fetched
things from the margins of the frame.
Bats caught in gauze curtains.

And the terror bled out over silver bowls
of floating rose petals.
In the background the fruits
grew heavy on the branches

and if you gaze at the photo
long enough you will see them drop
to the ground and rot, ooze nectar
and be covered with wasps.

Stay longer still and you will see
the grand costumes stiffen
and stand by themselves, empty,
echoing bird cries and the wind

tunneling through the immaculate sleeves.
The jungle grows up through them.
Vines invade the manor house
and the well scums over. Finally

the statues fall over by themselves
and the children play on them as if
they had never been more than piles of stones.

Town Meeting

They were defecating in public, he said,
and someone else said,
copulating, too,
and I thought, how many, a thousand?
All the homeless there are copulating in public? What a vision.
And then someone said,
not all the homeless
and we breathed easier,
only fifteen or so, and I thought
that's still a lot of them to be doing that in public
and by the time we were done
it was apparent
there had been only one each:
one copulation, one defecation,
and then someone else said,
you don't have to be homeless to do that.

Poverty

It gives you pigeon eyes,
makes you brave
as a cracked slate
with all the weight
of a house on top.

It bids you
hold out your quaky hand
through bittersweet temptations.

You dream of it as slick
silvery fish between your hands
wide eyed & breathless
but it circles your bleeding
feet like sharks.

At evening time
between lampposts & garbage
drums turned over in the wind,
poverty is black ice...
or a train, whose departure you miss,
whistling at you in the distance.

Your will is chalky on your tongue
like aspirin
& patience hangs like frayed
dreads down your back.

Morning bends
the scalpel-sharp pain
in the rib cage,
love's sulfur-dazed eyes.

Two tea bags in your wallet
for when the day is done
& poverty at your feet
like a hungry dog
laps up the sweat of your calves.
You come & go not speaking
fumbling for a ripcord
through a thousand leagues of wild wind.

Lawns

the magnolia tree I've claimed in full
April bloom & come visit
is in someone else's yard, has a surname
that corresponds to a playpen
of a parcel & its owner
and I think that lawns
are a concept of colonialist
empires, that hedges symbolize
prisons beautified
fences you cannot not cross

like straps for oxen they tighten
around the back of the eyes
of your soul, wrap & bear weight
leave open sores to become
the landing strips of flies

I have turned organic fences
& frontyards in my dreams
over & over — a country-full
and know they become walls
against their will

rebel by growing every
which way every so often
in the middle of the dark
that only blades can trim
their constant disobedience

Sweeping

This morning, in Fundeci
the breadman's basket weighed him
down & his call was a broken bird's.
This morning, the broom man came
at five a.m. crying *¡Escobas! ¡Escobas!* as if
he hadn't slept all night,
as if he had been crying *Sorrow! Murder!*
It is so many years before a war is over.

Yesterday, in Fundeci
a woman swept the front of her house,
hills reflected on the sweat
at the curve of her back,
and her boy, the boy
who dug up dead bullets from the swollen
earth of nearby yards, found one
he hammered into life.
It traveled between his eyes,
only blocks away from her.

This afternoon she sweeps
in long, steady strokes
as if she were crying
The heat! The sweltering heat!, meaning
to come up for air.

Nicaragua, 1991

The Night I Walk Into Town

The night I walk into town
to meet my brother
I'm tripped up
by a car whose wheels rip
through a newspaper
along the white line
of the road.
The black bold
type is bleeding.
I scream
but the bleeding doesn't stop.
At the corner a man who hasn't seen
water, food, gloved fingers
this cold, snow-blowing January
asks how many faces do I see
holding his chin up.
Twenty-five, I say
twenty-five thousand.

What's Happening

At this moment, fires of a riot are everywhere.
The men call into the smoke, We Want Justice!
Eyes blear from smoke.
In a cellblock the size of a moderate community church,
fifty, sixty fires are spewing everywhere.
My eyes are crying ....
the water is turned off, the air-conditioner off,
a sandwich for lunch, no breakfast, no supper,
the men scream, We Want Justice!
And this morning a Mexican is shot to death,
two weeks ago another Mexican was critically shot,
and the Black gangs are locked down,
the Chicanos and Whites are locked down,
and fires burn and burn before each cell,
voices scream and scream, We Want Justice!

The entire prison population quits working
in fields for three cents an hour,
in the factories for a dime an hour,
and fires engulf the tiers,
illuminate cell after cell
long deep eyes stare from.
Behind the flames and arms cloaked in smoke
is the cry, We Want Justice!
My cell fills with smoke, I can't see anyone or breathe,
and six hundred men cry, We Want Justice!
The fire! The Fire! And men cry out, Strike!
Viva La Huelga! La Huelga!
Music is playing above the flames, above the smoke,
and I am weeping with my hands over my face!
My cell fills with more smoke! I can't see the bars!
The whole cellblock is a huge billow of smoke!

Over the floor sewage reeks ankle high! Urine and feces!
Everywhere, flooding, and the water is turned off,
garbage piled up for weeks catches flames high! High!
Smoke and more smoke and more smoke!

No one can see anymore, but hear the raging cries,
Viva La Huelga! We Want Justice!
Men are screaming in their cells, behind the bars,
behind the smoke, flames and weeping, Men . . .
we live like this .... this is rehabilitation!
Grotesque Murderers! Ignorance! Waste and Blood!
Beatings! Robbery of Dignity! Sickness of Soul!

And through the smoke men's voices call,
how you doing over there? You OK?
And some yell, play the song I like, I love!
Play the one about the man that lost his woman!
About the one that fights for his freedom!
Through the smoke! The fire! The Murderers! Play! Play!
Let my soul feel once more the shudder of those days!
When I was free and human! Let me hear it and weep!
And the songs play, and the men sing along,
old sad faces and voices alive in the fire,
in the smoke and bars in their cells, they sing!

From far away in the night, you can see the big cellblock,
a sparking mountain of rock, jutting up, higher
than the mainyard walls, up, with six hundred men in it,
you can see the square windows filled red with fire,
from the flues on top of the roof shoot sparkles,
sprouts gray smoke,
at the windows red against the night flames jump,
pouring flames through broken windows,
expelling black gray smoke,
in the night surrounded with blackness,
and inside in the fire and smoke,
in foot deep sewage, are the cries, We Want Justice!

Viva La Huelga!
And the weeping, and the hate, and the blood!
And the despair, and rehabilitation!

Inside this furnace are the men, human beings, voices crying,
screaming and eyes weeping!
Poor Whites, poor Blacks, poor Chicanos, poor Indians,
who yell, turn the water on!
Let us flush our toilets! Let us drink some water!
They bang against the bars, shuddering rows of steel cages!

They bang against steel bars with broomsticks!
In the midst of flames and music and blood,
in shit and grime and smoke and scars and new wounds,
they scream, turn the water on!

And I am weeping! I am sick!
I have had enough, and yet every day I go on,
while this poem is read aloud by someone,
I am going on, and the sky is filling with black smoke,
the windows are filled with flames,
and I weep! My eyes burn! My lungs are black with smoke!

I Applied For The Board

...a flight of fancy and breath of fresh air
Is worth all the declines in the world.
It was funny though when I strode into the Board
And presented myself before the Council
With my shaggy-haired satchel, awiry
With ends of shoestrings and guitar strings
Holding it together, brimming with poems.

I was ready for my first grand, eloquent,
Booming reading of a few of my poems —
When the soft, surprised eyes
Of the chairman looked at me and said no.

And his two colleagues sitting on each side of him,
Peered at me through bluemetal eyes like rifle scopes,
And I like a deer in the forest heard the fresh,
Crisp twig break under my cautious feet,
As they surrounded me with quiet questions,
Closing in with grim sour looks, until I heard
The final shot burst from their mouths
That I had not made it, and felt the warm blood
Gush forth in my breast, partly from the wound,
And partly from the joy that it was over.

Who Understands Me But Me

They turn the water off, so I live without water,
they build walls higher, so I live without treetops,
they paint the windows black, so I live without sunshine,
they lock my cage, so I live without going anywhere,
they take each last tear I have, I live without tears,
they take my heart and rip it open, I live without heart,
they take my life and crush it, so I live without a future,
they say I am beastly and fiendish, so I have no friends,
they stop up each hope, so I have no passage out of hell,
they give me pain, so I live with pain,
they give me hate, so I live with my hate,
they have changed me, and I am not the same man,
they give me no shower, so I live with my smell,
they separate me from my brothers, so I live without brothers,
who understands me when I say this is beautiful?
who understands me when I say I have found other freedoms?

I cannot fly or make something appear in my hand,
I cannot make the heavens open or the earth tremble,
I can live with myself, and I am amazed at myself, my love,
my beauty,
I am taken by my failures, astounded by my fears,
I am stubborn and childish,
in the midst of this wreckage of life they incurred,
I practice being myself,
and I have found parts of myself never dreamed of by me,
they were goaded out from under rocks in my heart
when the walls were built higher,
when the water was turned off and the windows painted black.

I followed these signs
like an old tracker and followed the tracks deep into myself,
followed the blood-spotted path,

deeper into dangerous regions, and found so many parts of myself,
who taught me water is not everything,
and gave me new eyes to see through walls,
and when they spoke, sunlight came out of their mouths,
and I was laughing at me with them,
we laughed like children and made pacts to always be loyal,
who understands me when I say this is beautiful?

Ah Rain!

Sweet scented, dripping from eaves and darkening
plastered walls.
Muggy air! Goblet heavy and dark goldfish
filled with rain!
In the forehead of my brow is thunder!
My heart orange-colored,
my body an orange grove dripping with rain
and pungent with acids and roots, dead leaves,
thunder! thunder! thunder! in my forehead
lighting my darkened grove, shook branches
and petal dripping and bough snapping,
soft earth I plunge seeds to like sword tips,
in the crackle of sky my soul is,
in the sweeping winds, I lift my head high,
expand my chest to breathe! breathe! breathe!
breathe in the wood and green leaves,
in the musty earth, the rotten compositions
that create in their rot such famished beauty,
sweet and thick with life, dunked heavy
in rain, to swirl in our mouths life, life, life.
Body that I am, bone hard, black handed babe,
heart that I am, crushed raging aflame timber,
soul that I am, a hard chicken-pen dirt,
rain seeds, spitting down seeds,
the sun claws like a morning rooster.
The rain, rain, the rain, I put my head down,
so humble before my master Rain,
I drench my body, shimmer, clothes wet,
my religion is Rain, my anger, hate, love is Rain.

Steel Doors Of Prison

The big compound gates close the world off,
Lock with a thunderous thud and clunk,
While bits of dust scatter into your lungs,
Breathing in the first stark glance
Of prison cellblocks behind the great wall,
Breathing in the emptiness, the darkness
As you walk with an easy step on the cold sidewalk.

Then another door locks behind you.
This door is your cell door. A set of bars,
Paint scraped, still as cobras in gray skins,
Wrapping around your heart little by little:
The ones you love cannot be touched,
Christmas, Easter, Valentine's Day, Mother's Day,
All seen from these bars, celebrated
With a deep laboring yearning within,
While the cobras slowly wind and choke
Your mind, your heart, your spirit,
You hear nothing but the steel jaws close,
Slowly swallowing you . . .

La sangre de otros

Leo los poemas de los muertos
yo que estoy viva
yo que viví para reírme y llorar
y gritar Patria Libre o Morir
sobre un camión
el día que llegamos a Managua.

Leo los poemas de los muertos,
veo las hormigas sobre la grama,
mis pies descalzos,
tu pelo lacio,
espalda encorvada sobre la reunión.

Leo los poemas de los muertos
y siento que esta sangre con que nos amamos,
no nos pertenece.

The Blood of Others

I read the poems of the dead.
I survived.
I lived to laugh and cry
and I shouted *Patria Libre o Morir*
from the back of a truck
the day we reached Managua.

I read the poems of the dead,
watching the ants on the grass,
my bare feet,
your straight hair,
your back arched at the meeting.

I read the poems of the dead.
Does the blood in our bodies that lets us love each other
belong to us?

translated by Steven F. White

In Memoriam

Como una inmensa catedral,
ahumada de tiempo y peregrinos,
abierta de vitrales,
cobijada de musgo y pequeñas violetas olorosas,
esta noche oficio para vos,
un *In Memoriam* cálido,
una lámpara ardiendo.

Por los más oscuros pasadizos de mis muros internos,
a través de intrincados laberintos,
de puertas canceladas,
de candados y rejas,
camino hacia el encuentro de tu sombra.
Tu efigie de largas vestiduras monacales
me espera en el atrio del recuerdo
junto a la fuente silenciada.

Arrastro las largas vestiduras del encierro.
No sé si notarás,
cuando callada te me acerque,
cómo mi corazón semeja un cirio
y cómo se me amontonan en los ojos
todas las mieles espesas de la sangre.

En el redondo espacio temporal
de esta noche en que invoco tu nombre,
alzo el manto que oculta quedamente el secreto,
te muestro el altar de los suspiros,
la caja cincelada donde guardo tus gestos,
el conjuro de rosas que perfuma mis huesos.

Mi cuerpo tu perenne habitación.
Tu morada de las suaves paredes.

In Memoriam

Like an immense cathedral,
filled with the incense of time and pilgrims,
my stained-glass windows open,
covered with moss and fragrant tiny violets,
ardently, tonight,
I celebrate for you
a burning *In Memoriam*.

Through the darkest passageways of my innermost walls,
crossing winding labyrinths
doors boarded shut,
locks and bars,
I walk towards your shadow.
Dressed in long monastic robes,
your image awaits in the atrium of memory
by the silenced fountain.

I trail the long robes of confinement.
Perhaps you will not notice,
as I quietly approach you,
the way my heart resembles a ceremonial candle
and how blood and thick honey
rush together, melting, in my eyes.

In the round, temporal space of this night,
where I invoke your name
I raise the veil that deftly guards the secret:
I bestow upon you the altar of sighs,
the carved box where I keep your gestures,
the spell of roses that perfumes my bones.

My body, your perennial abode
Walled realm gently enclosing you.

Quizás ya no recuerdes
cómo ocupabas sus entrañas,
sus celdas enrejadas,
pero ellas conocen los murmullos, los cánticos.
Basta una chispa y lo muerto revive,
lo que pensábase dormido, despierta.

Oficio así esta resurrección,
este rito de invierno,
abierta, florecida como las limonarias.
Te enrostro mi amor enclaustrado,
sepultado tras días y barrotes de acero,
este amor sumergido tras pétalos de agua,
conservado en archivos subterráneos
lapidado, proscrito, negado miles veces,
intacto zarzal sin consumirse,
delicado reducto que la sangre preserva.
Lo pongo de nuevo en su lugar,
en su jaula del jardín de maduras manzanas,
lo condeno otra vez a la ceguera, lo silencio.

Ya mañana
trataré de olvidar
que, de luto, esta noche
me habitaste de nuevo
y fui aquella mujer que te llamaba
sin que jamás tu voz le respondiera.

Perhaps you don't remember
how you used to dwell inside its caves,
its rooms with barred windows,
but they remember the murmuring, the canticles.
Light one spark and ashes come to life,
what appeared asleep
suddenly comes awake.

And so I celebrate this resurrection,
this springtime ritual,
blossoming, opening, like lemon flowers.
I confront you with my cloistered love,
this love submerged under petals of water,
kept away in underground vaults,
buried alive, banned, denied a thousand times,
burning bush that never turns to ash,
delicate recess nourished by blood.
Then I return it to where it belongs,
to its cage in the garden of ripened apples,
again I condemn it to blindness, I silence it.

Come tomorrow,
I shall try to forget
that tonight,
in mourning,
you inhabited me again
and I was once more that woman
calling your name in vain.

translated by Steven F. White

Conjunción

Afuera
la noche agazapada
aguarda como tigre
el salto mortal a través de la ventana;
en este recinto donde doliosamente
hago surgir del aire las palabras
me asombra la latente presencia de un beso sobre la pierna.
No hay nadie: sólo mi cuerpo solo,
mi cuerpo y los cabellos extendidos en imágenes
estoy yo y están ellas
las mujeres sin habla
esas que mis dedos alumbran
esas que la noche se lleva en su aliento de luna.

Mújeres de los siglos me habitan:
Isadora bailando con su túnica
Virginia Woolf, su cuarto propio
Safo lanzándose desde la roca;
Medea, Fedra, Jane Eyre
y mis amigas
espantando lo viejo del tiempo
escribiéndose a sí mismas
sacudiendo las sombras para alumbrar sus perfiles
y dejarse ver por fin
desnudadas de toda convención.

Mujeres danzan a la luz de mi lámpara
se suben a las mesas, dicen discursos incendiarios
me sitian con los sufrimientos
las marcas del cuerpo el alumbramiento de los hijos
el silencio de las olorosas cocinas los
efímeros tensos dormitorios.

Conjunction

Outside
the crouching night
waits like a tiger
to do a somersault through the window
within these walls where painfully
I make the words emerge from the air,
the latent presence of a kiss on my leg surprises me.
There is no one. Only my body alone.
My body and my hair extended in images.
I am here and so are they
the speechless women
the ones my fingers illuminate
the ones the night's moon-breath carries.

Women of the centuries inhabit me:
Isadora dancing with her tunic
Virginia Woolf, a room of her own,
Sappho throwing herself from the rock;
Medea, Phaedra, Jane Eyre
and my women-friends
scaring time's aging
writing themselves
shaking off the shadows to pour light on their faces
and being seen at last
stripped of all convention.

Women dance by the light of my lamp,
climb onto the tables, give incendiary speeches
besiege me with their suffering
the bruises on their bodies the pain of childbirth
the silence of the fragrant kitchens
the ephemeral tense bedrooms.

Mujeres enormes monumentos me circundan
dicen sus poemas cantan bailan recuperan la voz;
dicen: No pude estudiar latín: no pude
escribir como Shakespeare;
nadie se apiadó de mi gusto por la música;
George Sand: tuve que disfrazarme de hombre;
escribí oculta en el nombre masculino.
Y más allá Jane Austen, acomodando las
palabras de "Orgullo y Prejuicio"
en un cuaderno en la sala común de la parroquia
interrumpida innumerablemente por los visitantes.

Mujeres de los siglos adustas envejecidas tiernas
con los ojos brillantes descienden a mi entorno
ellas perecederas inmortales
parecieran gozar detrás de las pestañas
viendo mi cuarto propio
el nítido legajo de papeles blancos
el moderno electrónico computador
los estantes de libros
los gruesos diccionarios
el cenicero negro de ceniza
el humo del cigarro.

Yo miro los armarios con la ropa blanca
las pequeñas y suaves prendas íntimas
la lista del mercado en la mesa de noche;
siento la necesidad de un beso sobre la pierna.

Great women monumental women encircle me
they recite their poems sing dance win back their voices;
they say: I couldn't study Latin: I couldn't
write like Shakespeare;
no one took pity on my love for music;
George Sand: I had to disguise myself as a man;
I wrote hidden behind a masculine name.
And beyond, Jane Austen placing the
words of "Pride and Prejudice"
in a notebook in the common room of the parish
endlessly interrupted by visitors.

Sober, aged, gentle women of the centuries,
with shining eyes, come down to surround me
these perishable immortal women
glance around my room with pleasure.
They see the neat pile of white paper,
the modern electronic word processor
the shelves of books
the thick dictionaries
the ashtray black with ashes
the cigarette smoke.

I look at the linen closet
the soft and silky underwear in the drawer
the shopping list on the night table;
I still feel like I need a kiss on my leg.

translated by Steven F. White

Incoming

Don't let them kid you—
The mind no fool like the movies,
doesn't wait for flash or screech,
but moves of its own accord,
even hears the slight
bump the mortars make
as they kiss the tubes good-bye.
Then the furious rain,
a fist driving home a message:
"Boy, you don't belong here."
On good nights they walk them in.
You wait for them to fall,
stomach pinned so tight to ground
you might feel a woman's foot
pace a kitchen floor in Brownsville;
the hushed fall of a man lost
in a corn field in Michigan;
a young girl's finger trace
her lover's name on a beach on Cape Cod.
But then the air is sucked
straight up off the jungle
floor and the entire weight
of Jupiter and her moons
presses down on the back of a knee.
In a moment, it's over.
But it takes a lifetime to recover,
let out the last breath
you took as you dove.
This is why you'll see them sometimes,
in malls, men and women off in corners:
the ways they stare through windows in silence.

Playing Basketball with the Viet Cong

for Nguyên Quáng Sang

You never thought it would come to this,
that afternoon in the war
when you leaned so hard into the controls
you became part of the landscape:
just you, the old man, old woman
and their buffalo.
You never thought then
that this gray-haired man in sandals
smoking Gauloises on your back porch,
drinking your beer, his rough cough
punctuating tales of how he fooled
the French in '54,
would arrive at your back door
to call you out to shoot baskets, friend.
If at first he seems awkward,
before long he's got it down.
His left leg lifts from the ground,
his arms arch back then forward
from the waist to release the ball
arcing to the hoop, one, two, . . .
ten straight times. You stare at him
in his tee shirt, sandals, and shorts.
Yes, he smiles. It's a gift,
good for bringing gunships down
as he did in the Delta
and in other places where, he whispers,
there may be other scores to settle.

Gelatin Factory

No need to look for the place,
just follow your nose,
the man at unemployment
said, not sure he was joking.
Down where the river turned
and the factory rose,
there were always jobs
on the night shift.
Only you and the foreman
knew English.
Not Héctor and José,
who punched in late
those summer nights
from bars still cursing
women, baseball and the Colombians.
Maybe it was nostalgia
for the heat that brought them.
Never less than 100 degrees
on the catwalks, more near
the ovens. And all summer
men of many colors dying
in jungles and cities of Asia.
But only pigs died here.
You didn't believe at first,
but saw the evidence:
morning, freight cars,
loaded like ships to the gunnels
with carcasses of dead piglets,
pulled onto the sidings.
All day, their small, twisted bodies
grayed in the sun, legs
pointed to the heavens
that failed them.

No farmer to claim
the honor of this crop,
raised to be boiled in acid,
rendered a sticky mass
rolled on screens and cooked
in sheets to glass, smashed
and ground to a fine powder
useful for many things
but best for those sweet desserts,
late on Sundays, children
circled and ate.

In the Village of Yen So

After the dust of the village brick factory,
she offers tea,
bitter green oranges for respite.

Numbers tumble in our heads:
how many commune members
comprise how many families

sharing how many hectares of land
producing how many tons of rice,
fish, maize, bricks, carpets,

piglets, and yes, children,
like the boy who peers in
at the door.

In silence we scribble facts
into notebooks. Nguyen Thi Chu
quietly moves about the tables

serving tea, her mind fixed on other numbers.
Fifteen years ago. Christmas Day. The guns,
the arcing lights, then rush of flares.

Two hundred fifty eight killed that night.
Five hundred who went south to war.
Two hundred and sixteen who didn't return.
She remembers the names, the eyes,
wishes we could see them
as she does, staring in at the door.

Banking Lesson, 1970

Your hero's welcome was cleaning
floors at the local bank
for minimum wage.
A little joke to start the day,
leaning on a pole, a train
rumbling through a tunnel,
a blue janitor's uniform from Sears
replacing olive green.
You were reading Stendhal,
stuck in your back pocket like a confession.
Each day, seven A.M., you began your tour
sweeping tape across the computer room,
everyone watching, you could tell.
Knock first before checking
the washrooms for paper stock,
empty trash pails for executives.
If they knew the murder in your head....
Lunch was a cafeteria filled
with girls in six-inch heels
and men in blue suits.
You ached as you passed through the line.
Back by the loading docks
you smoked your wrath up,
watched armored trucks bring
the day's deposits from the branches.
How far could you get, you wondered,
Wednesdays mopping the main vault,
stacks of bills rising in piles on the walls.
How far?

Non Vedra Mai Piu Forse

Un mio compagno oggi in fabbrica
        ha perso un occhio
            con uno spruzzo
            di soda caustica.
Non è escluso che resti cieco.
Non vedrà mai più forse
            il cielo e la terra.
Nessuno di noi più
            potrà guardare in volto
            compagni
non vedrà mai più forse alcun giorno.
Nuova solitudine,
nuovo carico di agghiacciante dolore.
Il nostro cuore, tutto il nostro cuore forse
            sarà lanciato via così
                per sempre
dentro uno straccio inzuppato, nero d'olio.

Maybe He'll Never See Again

A buddy of mine in the factory today
   lost an eye
    when some caustic
    substance got sprayed.
It's possible he could be blind.
He may never again see
    the sky and the land.
None of us can
    look the comrades in the face
    anymore;
he may never again see another day.
So it's new loneliness,
a new load of hair-raising sorrow.
Maybe our heart, our whole heart will be
    likewise tossed away
     forever
inside a soaking rag black with oil.

translated by Jack Hirschman

Non Ditemi Di Non Disturbarvi

Blocchi giganti di cemento
    grandi intelaiature di ferro
      lunghi tubi
si sono accampati sul mio sangue.
La polvere, il ferro, gli asfalti
mi hanno ricoperto tutta l'anima.
I miei occhi sono appesi
    a densi funghi gialli
      velenosi
che premono di continuo contro il cielo.
Non ditemi di non chiamarvi,
      di non disturbarvi.
Nelle mie carni si sentono solo
      lunghe grida di sirene
    stridori di lamiere
      rumori aspri.
Le ciminiere sono ferite, crateri
      profondl aperti
        sul mio corpo.
Non ditemi di lasciarvi in pace.
La morte si sta accanendo
      contro la vita.
La morte è tutta scoperta.
Non ditemi che non vi interessa.
Non ditemi che non vi interessa.

Don't Tell Me Not To Bother You

Giant cement blocks
      huge iron scaffoldings
           long pipes
are camped in my blood.
Dust, iron and asphalt
have covered my whole soul.
My eyes are heavy
      with thick, poisonously yellow
           mushroom clouds
pressing directly against the sky.
Don't tell me not to call on you,
      not to bother you.
What I'm hearing in my flesh is
      long siren-wails
    armor-plated shrieks
      cutting noises.
The smoke-stacks are wounds, deep
      craters open
        on my body.
Don't tell me to leave you alone.
Death's working like a dog
      against life.
Death's laid bare.
Don't tell me you're not interested.
Don't tell me you're not interested.

translated by Jack Hirschman

A Julia de Burgos

Ya las gentes murmuran que yo soy tu enemiga
porque dicen que en verso doy al mundo tu yo.

Mienten, Julia de Burgos. Mienten, Julia de Burgos.
La que se alza en mis versos no es tu voz: es mi voz
porque tú eres ropaje y la esencia soy yo;
y el más profundo abismo se tiende entre las dos.

Tú eres fría muñeca de mentira social,
y yo, viril destello de la humana verdad.

Tú, miel de cortesanas hipocresías; yo no;
que en todos mis poemas desnudo el corazón.

Tú eres como tu mundo, egoísta; yo no;
que en todo me lo juego a ser lo que soy yo.

Tú eres sólo la grave señora señorona;
yo no; yo soy la vida, la fuerza, la mujer.

Tú eres de tu marido, de tu amo; yo no;
yo de nadie, o de todos, porque a todos, a todos,
en mi limpio sentir y en mi pensar me doy.

Tú te rizas el pelo y te pintas; yo no;
a mí me riza el viento; a mí me pinta el sol.

Tú eres dama casera, resignada, sumisa,
atada a los prejuicios de los hombres; yo no;
que yo soy Rocinante corriendo desbocado
olfateando horizontes de justicia de Dios.

To Julia de Burgos

Already the people murmur that I am your enemy
Because they say that in verse I give the world your me.

They lie, Julia de Burgos. They lie, Julia de Burgos.
Who rises in my verses is not your voice. It is my voice
Because you are the dressing and the essence is me;
And the most profound abyss is spread between us.

You are the cold doll of social lies,
And I, the virile starburst of the human truth.

You, honey of courtesan hypocrisies; not me;
In all my poems I undress my heart.

You are like your world, selfish; not me
Who gambles everything betting on what I am.

You are only the ponderous lady very lady;
not me; I am life, strength, woman.

You belong to your husband, your master; not me;
I belong to nobody, or all, because to all, to all
I give myself in my clean feeling and in my thought.

You curl your hair and paint yourself; not me;
the wind curls my hair, the sun paints me.

You are a housewife, resigned, submissive,
tied to the prejudices of men; not me;
Unbridled, I am a runaway Rocinante
snorting horizons of God's justice.

Tú en ti misma no mandas; a ti todos te mandan;
en ti mandan tu esposo, tus padres, tus parientes,
el cura, la modista, el teatro, el casino,
el auto, las alhajas, el banquete, el champán,
el cielo y el infierno, y el qué dirán social.

En mí no, que en mí manda mi solo corazón,
mi solo pensamiento; quien manda en mí soy yo.

Tú, flor de aristocracia; y yo, la flor del pueblo.
Tú en ti lo tienes todo y a todos se lo debes,
mientras que yo, mi nada a nadie se la debo.

Tú, clavada al estático dividendo ancestral,
y yo, un uno en la cifra del divisor social,
somos el duelo a muerte que se acerca fatal.

Cuando las multitudes corran alborotadas
dejando atrás cenizas de injusticias quemadas,
y cuando con la tea de las siete virtudes,
tras los siete pecados, corran las multitudes,
contra ti, y contra todo lo injusto y lo inhumano,
yo iré en medio de ellas con la tea en la mano.

You in yourself have no say; everyone governs you;
your husband, your parents, your family,
the priest, the dressmaker, the theater, the dance hall,
the auto, the fine furnishings, the feast, champagne,
heaven and hell, and the social, "what will they say."

Not in me, in me my only heart governs,
my only thought; who governs in me is me.

You, flower of aristocracy; and me, flower of the people.
You in you have everything and you owe it to everyone,
while me, my nothing I owe to nobody.

You, nailed to the static ancestral dividend,
and me, a one in the numerical social divider,
we are the duel to death who fatally approaches.

When the multitudes shall run rioting
leaving behind ashes of burned injustices,
and with the torch of the seven virtues,
the multitude will run after the seven sins,
against you and against everything unjust and inhuman,
I will be in their midst with the torch in my hand.

translated by Jack Agüeros

Las voces de los muertos

En España

Fué en un alba en Madrid, donde inicié mi ruta
por esta tierra negra de tiniebla y gusanos.
Recuerdo que al caer, una furia de vendas
arrebató mis ojos a mis vencidos párpados.
¿Se borraron también, prematuros y frágiles,
en la siniestra boca que le abrieron al campo?
Fué ese mismo demonio de las alas hinchadas
que me partió; miradme, profundo y fragmentado.
Fué ese mismo que humilla las pupilas del cielo:
que se nutre de crimen y arrozales quemados
que se roba la vida y se traga ciudades;
está suelto; cogedle; no más tumbas, hermanos.
¡Mi guitarra! ¡Mis ojos! ¡Mis canciones! ¡Mi España!
¿Dónde estáis? ¡Esta venda! ¡Asesinos! ¡Malvados!
Si es preciso, en gusanos subiré a sonreirte
la infernal maldición de tus muertos, ¡Oh Franco!

En La China

¡Chiang Kai Shek! ¿Y mis huesos? ¿Y mi cara sin ojos?
¿Y mis manos erguidas de esperanza y trabajo?
¿Y mis pies sin caminos que una vez fueron alas?
¿Y mis huellas, mi sangre, mis caídos pedazos?
¿Dónde están? ¿En qué furia de claveles se duermen?
¿En qué sol fortifican sus harapos mojados?
¿Qué misterio se nutre de mi ausencia profunda?
¡Un recuerdo, una luz, de que un día fuí humano!
Estoy solo, vacío, separado y ausente;
confundido, sin sitio, voy buscando mi rastro.
¿No hubo suelo en el mundo para enterrar el crimen?

The Voices Of The Dead

In Spain

It was in a dawn in Madrid, where I started my passage
through this black earth of darkness and worms.
I remember that upon falling, a fury of bandages
snatched my eyes from my defeated eyelids.
Were they also erased, premature and fragile,
in the sinister mouth that opened to the countryside?
It was that same demon of the swollen wings
that split me; look at me, profound and fragmented.
It was the same one that humiliates the pupils of heaven;
who is nourished by crime and burned rice fields
who steals life and swallows cities,
it is loose—catch it; no more tombs, brothers.
My guitar! My eyes! My songs! My Spain!
Where are you? This blindfold! Assassins! Wicked!
If necessary, in worms I will rise to smile at
the infernal malediction of your dead, Oh Franco!

In China

Chiang Kai Shek! And my bones? And my face without eyes?
And my hands raised in hope and work?
And my feet without paths that once were wings?
And my prints, my blood, my fallen pieces?
Where are they? In what fury of carnations do they sleep?
In what sun do they fortify their wet rags?
What mystery is nourished by my profound absence?
A memory, a light, that one day I was human!
I am alone, empty, separate and absent;
confused, graveless, I am looking for my trail.
Wasn't there room on the earth to bury the crime?

¡Ni siquiera una tumba, miserables, avaros!
Pero no; fué una tumba allá abajo en Madrid.
¿Por qué aqui voy sin tumba? ¿Dónde estoy? ¿Y mis párpados?
¿Por qué voy con un nombre abanderando el aire?
¿Chiang Kai Shek, en que idioma te saludan los pájaros?
Debe ser nombre alto ese tuyo, solemne,
y familiar, y mío; ya te recuerdo, hermano;
si no fué ni en España, ni en un alba, ni roto
como entré por la muerte; fué en la China, quemado.
Y aquí mismo, en la China, sin sepulcro, sin huesos,
me quedaré en tus filas, General, esperando;
y te ofrezco, certera, para alzar la victoria,
mi voz de muerto libre, satisfecho y vengado.

En los mares Britanicos

Mis islas, a distancia, apagándose en mí,
bajo un cielo de bombas y terror estrellado.
¿Será la muerte allí más humana y más breve;
será más clara y honda que en este ronco charco?
Corriendo, sin miradas, anegado de azules;
entre metralla y ola, silenciado en pedazos;
no verse la amplia sangre remozando caminos;
no sentirse los ojos arropados de llanto.
¡Soledad de la guerra, rabiosa soledad
localizada en este remolino océanico
humillado en un trágico sepulcro de corrientes;
finito y solo en tanto infinito azulado!
¡Oh no saber morir, mantenerse despierto
cuando sólo nos quedan unos huesos mojados!
¿Será la muerte allí más humana y más breve;
en mis islas inglesas, bajo aquel cielo falso?

En los trigales Rusos

Yo estaba en los trigales, en la risa del hombre,
en la fábrica alegre, en la luz del trabajo;

Not even a tomb, miserable, avaricious!
But no, it was a tomb way down in Madrid.
Why am I here without a tomb? Where am I? And my eyelids?
Why do I travel with a name flagging the air?
Chiang Kai Shek, in what language do the birds greet you?
It must be a mighty name yours; solemn,
and familiar, and mine; I remember you now, brother;
it wasn't in Spain, nor in a dawning, nor broken
how I entered death, it was in China, burned.
And right here, in China, without a sepulchre without bones
I will remain in your ranks, General, waiting;
and I offer you, with certainty, to raise victory,
with my voice of the free dead, satisfied and avenged.

On The British Seas

My islands, at a distance, extinguishing in me,
under a sky of bombs and shattered terror.
Can death there be more human and more brief;
can it be clearer and deeper than in this hoarse puddle?
Running, without looking, swamped in blues;
between machine gun and wave, silenced in pieces,
not seeing one's ample blood rejuvenating paths;
not feeling one's eyes blanketed with weeping!
Solitude of war, rabid solitude,
located in this oceanic whirlpool
humiliated in a tragic sepulchre of currents;
finite and alone in so much bluish infinite!
Oh to not know how to die, keeping awake
when only a few wet bones are left of us!
Can death there be more human and more brief
on my English islands, beneath that false sky?

In The Russian Wheatfields

I was in the wheatfields, in the laughter of man,
in the happy factory, in the light of work;

el sol me amanecía y el capullo me alzaba,
y en mis manos el día era ruta de cantos.
A mi lado, la espiga florecía claridades,
el hombre cosechaba la justicia en sus campos;
la verdad respiraba del pulmón de la tierra,
y en un sólo camino se apretaban mis pasos.
Era yo el universo liberado, sencillo,
que iba entonces, sin miedo, sobre Rusia cruzando.
¡Cómo recuerdo el alma de canción de los niños,
y la blanca confianza del dolor levantado!
Pero un día mis miradas se poblaron de tumbas;
mi alegría se hizo un cañón en mis manos;
algún monstruo era suelto por la selva del hombre,
y una sola palabra se imponía: aplastarlo.
Con tanta vida abierta por los surcos subiendo,
preferir un sepulcro a pactar; morir alto;
despedazarse, herirse con todos los caminos,
pero jamás doblarse a la sed de los bárbaros.
Yo estaba en los trigales, en la risa del hombre,
en la fábrica alegre, en la luz del trabajo.
Un día mis miradas se poblaron de tumbas,
y yo, tumba entre ellas, todavía voy sembrando.

En las filas Alemanas

¡Dejadme entrar, hermanos, por el gran cementerio!
Fuí nacido, crecido para matar; mis párpados
jamás se sonrieron con el ansia de un niño
ni una estrella rendida de mi emoción fué blanca.
Aurora de uniformes; juventud de uniformes;
crepúsculo de oscuros uniformes manchados;
la visión fija en fijos paisajes de venganza;
la razón muerta en tétrico apetito macabro.
Desolado, fugado de mí mismo, perdido
en una soledad erizada de espanto...
Así fué que caí, agotado de nada,
en la trágica muerte del que nunca fué humano.

the sun awoke me and the bud roused me,
and in my hands the day was a route of cantos.
At my side the stalk flowered daylights,
man reaped justice in his fields,
the truth breathed from the lung of the earth,
and in one sole path my steps were tightened.
I was the universe liberated, simple
that was then fearlessly crossing over Russia.
How I remember the soul song of the children,
and the white confidence of the lifted pain!
But one day my sight was populated by tombs;
my happiness became a cannon in my hands;
some monster was loose in the woods of man,
and only one phrase imposed itself: flatten it.
With so much open life rising through the furrows,
I preferred a sepulchre to a deal; to die tall;
break into pieces, wound oneself with all the paths,
but never bow to the thirst of barbarians.
I was in the wheatfields, in that laughter of man,
in the happy factory, in the light of work.
One day my sight was populated by tombs,
and I, tomb among them, am still planting.

In The German Ranks

Let me enter, brothers, through the great cemetery!
I was born, raised, to kill; my eyelids
never smiled with the desire of a child
not one surrendered star of my emotion was white.
Aurora of uniforms, youth of uniforms,
twilight of dark uniforms stained;
the vision fixed in fixed landscapes of vengeance;
the reason dead in gloomy macabre appetite.
Desolate, escaped from myself, lost
in a solitude bristling with fright...
Thus I fell, exhausted from nothing,
in the tragic death of who was never human.

Así fué que caí, en la misma metralla
que forjó mi pasión, orientada en lo insano.
Desertor de las filas que borraron mi nombre
en un épico salto olvidé mi pasado.
¡Dejadme entrar, hermanos, por el gran cementerio!
¡Yo soy entre los muertos el más grande, el más trágico;
ya que no tuve nunca un mundo entre los vivos,
un mundo entre los muertos ofrecedme, soldados!

El muerto universal

¿Y quien soy yo? ¿Qué busco por la orilla del hombre?
¿Dónde fué que caí? ¿Con qué enseña arropado?
¿Y ese inmenso horizonte de sepulcros que marchan?
¡Todos los muertos quieren una ruta en mi paso!
Hombre vivo, detente de tu orgía de metrallas;
por un instante mirate en mi rostro de espanto;
soy el más gigantesco de los muertos, que nunca
te cerrará los ojos hasta verte salvado.

Thus I fell, in the same machine gun
that forged my passion, oriented to the insane.
Deserter of the ranks that erased my name
in an epic leap I forgot my past.
Let me enter brothers, through the great cemetery!
Among the dead, I am the greatest, the most tragic;
soldiers, since I never had a world among the living
offer me a world among the dead!

The Universal Dead

And who am I? What do I look for at the edge of man?
Where did I fall? Wrapped in what ensign?
And that immense horizon of marching sepulchres?
All the dead want a passage in my steps!
Man alive, stop your orgy of machine guns;
for an instant look at yourself in my face of fright;
I am the most gigantic of the dead who will never
close his eyes until I see you saved.

translated by Jack Agüeros

Ecología

En septiembre por San Ubaldo se vieron más coyotes.
Más cuajipales, a poco del triunfo,
en los ríos, allá por San Ubaldo.
En la carretera más conejos, culumucos ...
La población de pájaros se ha triplicado, nos dicen,
en especial la de los piches.
Los bulliciosos piches bajan a nadar adonde ven el agua brillar.
Los somocistas también destruían los lagos, ríos, y montañas.
Desviaban el curso de los ríos para sus fincas.
El Ochomogo se había secado el verano pasado.
El Sinecapa secado por el despale de los latifundistas.
El Río Grande de Matagalpa, secado, durante la guerra,
allá por los llanos de Sébaco.
Dos represas pusieron al Ochomogo,
y los desechos químicos capitalistas
caían en el Ochomogo y los pescados andaban como borrachos.
El río de Boaco con aguas negras.
La laguna de Moyuá se había secado. Un coronel somocista
robó las tierras de los campesinos, y construyó una represa.
La laguna de Moyuá que por siglos estuvo bella en ese sitio.
(Pero ya volverán los pescaditos).
Despalaron y represaron.
Pocos garrobos al sol, pocos cusucos.
La tortuga verde del Caribe la vendía Somoza.
En camiones exportaban los huevos de paslama y las iguanas.
Acabándose la tortuga caguama.
El pez-sierra del Gran Lago acabándolo José Somoza.
En peligro de extinción el tigrillo de la selva,
su suave piel color de selva,
y el puma, el danto en las montañas
(como los campesinos en las montañas).
¡Y pobre el Río Chiquito! Su desgracia,

Ecology

You saw more coyotes near San Ubaldo in September.
And more alligators, a little after the triumph,
   in the rivers, there near San Ubaldo.
      More rabbits and raccoons on the road...
The bird population has tripled, they say,
   especially the *piches*.
The noisy *piches* go swim wherever they see the water shining.
The Somocistas destroyed the lakes, rivers, and mountains too.
   They diverted the course of the rivers for their farms.
The Ochomogo had dried up last summer.
The Sinecapa dried up because the landowners stripped the land.
The Río Grande of Matagalpa dried up during the war,
      there near the Sebaco Plains.
They built two dams on the Ochomogo,
         and the capitalist chemical wastes
spilled into the Ochomogo and the fish reeled around like drunks.
      The Boaco River carried sewage.
The Moyuá Lagoon dried up. A Somocista colonel
robbed the peasants' land and built a dam.
The Moyuá Lagoon that for centuries had been beautiful in that spot.
     (But the little fish will soon return.)
They stripped the land and built dams.
        Few *garrobos* in the sun, few armadillos.
Somoza sold the Caribbean green tortoise.
They exported *paslama* and iguana eggs by the truckload.
     The caguama tortoise finished.
The Gran Lago swordfish finished off by José Somoza.
Facing danger of extinction the jungle jaguar,
   its soft skin the color of the jungle,
and the puma, the tapir in the mountains
        (like the peasants in the mountains).
And the poor Chiquito River! Its misfortune

la de todo el país. Reflejado en sus aguas el somocismo.
El Río Chiquito de León, alimentado de manantiales
de cloacas, desechos de fábricas de jabón y curtiembres,
agua blanca de fábricas de jabón, roja la de las curtiembres;
plásticos en el lecho, vacinillas, hierros sarrosos. Eso
nos dejó el somocismo.
(Hay que verlo otra vez bonito y claro cantando hacia el mar).
Y al lago de Managua todas las aguas negras de Managua
y los desechos químicos.
        Y allá por Solentiname, en la isla La Zanata:
un gran cerro blanco y hediondo de esqueletos de pez-sierra.
Pero ya respiraron los pez-sierra y el tiburón de agua dulce.
Tisma está llena otra vez de garzas reales
                        reflejadas en sus espejos.
Tiene muchos zanatillos, piches, güises, zarcetas.
        La flora también se ha beneficiado.
Los cusucos andan muy contentos con este gobierno.
        Recuperaremos los bosques, ríos, lagunas.
Vamos a descontaminar el lago de Managua.
La liberación no soló la ansiaban los humanos.
Toda la ecología gemía. La revolución
es también de lagos, ríos, árboles, animales.

that of the whole country. Somocismo reflected in its waters.
The Chiquito River of León, fed by brooks
of sewage, soap factory and tannery wastes,
white water from the soap factories, red from the tanneries;
plastics, chamber pots, rusty iron in the riverbed. This
is what Somocismo left us.
(We have to see the river pretty and clear once again singing its way to
the sea).
And into Lake Managua all of Managua's waste waters
and chemical wastes.
And there near Solentiname, on La Zanata Island:
a great white stinking heap of swordfish skeletons.
But the swordfish and freshwater sharks are breathing again.
Tisma is full of royal herons again
reflected in its mirrors.
It has many little starlings, *piches, güises,* widgets.
The plant life has benefited too.
The armadillos are very happy with this government.
We will restore our forests, rivers, lagoons.
We will decontaminate Lake Managua.
Not only humans longed for liberation.
All ecology groaned for it also. The revolution
is also one of lakes, rivers, trees, animals.

translated by Marc Zimmerman

Las loras

Mi amigo Michel es responsable militar en Somoto,
        allá por la frontera con Honduras,
y me contó que descubrió un contrabando de loras
que iban a ser exportadas a EE. UU.
            para que allí aprendieran a hablar inglés.
Eran 186 loras, y ya habían muerto 47 en sus jaulas.
Y él las regresó al lugar de donde las habían traído,
y cuando el camión estaba llegando a un lugar
                    que llaman Los Llanos
cerea de las montañas de donde eran esas loras
        (las montañas se veían grandes
                    detrás de esos llanos)
las loras comenzaron a agitarse y a batir sus alas
 y a apretujarse contra las paredes de sus jaulas.
Y cuando les abrieron las jaulas
todas volaron como flechas en la misma dirección
                        a sus montañas.
Eso mismo hizo la Revolución con nosotros, pienso yo:
nos sacó de las jaulas
                en las que nos llevaban a hablar inglés.
Nos devolvió la patria de la que nos habían arrancado.

Los compas verdes como loras
                dieron a las loras sus montañas verdes.
        Pero hubo 47 que murieron.

The Parrots

My friend Michel is the military leader in Somoto,
                    there near the border with Honduras,
and he told me he discovered a contraband shipment of parrots
set for export to the U.S.
                    so that there they would learn to speak English.
There were 186 parrots, and 47 had already died in their cages.
And he sent them back where they'd come from,
and when the truck reached a place
                    they call The Plains
near the mountain homes of these parrots
                    (the mountains looked huge
                                rising from these plains)
the parrots began to stir and beat their wings
                    and jam themselves against their cage walls.
And when the cages were opened
they all flew out like arrows in the same direction
                                toward their mountains.
This is the same thing, I think, that the Revolution did to us:
it took us out of the cages
                    in which they'd carried us off to speak English.
It brought us back the homeland from which they'd uprooted us.

The soldiers green like parrots
                    gave the parrots their green mountains.
        But there were 47 who died.

translated by Marc Zimmerman

Las campesinas del Cuá

Voy a hablarles ahora de los gritos del Cuá
    gritos de mujeres como de parto
María Venancia de 90 años, sorda, casi cadáver
    grita a los guardias no he visto muchachos
la Amanda Aguilar de 50 años
       con sus hijitas Petrona y Erlinda
       no he visto muchachos
como de parto
—Tres meses en un cuartel de montaña—
Angela García de 25 y siete menores
    La Cándida de 16 años amamanta una niñita
      muy diminuta y desnutrida
Muchos han oído estos gritos del Cuá
      gemidos de la Patria como de parto
Al salir de la cárcel Estebana García con cuatro menores
dio a luz. Tuvo que regalar sus hijos
    a un finquero. Emelinda Hernández de 16
        las mejillas brillantes de llanto
    las trenzas mojadas de llanto …
Capturadas en Tazua cuando venían de Waslala
    la milpa en flor y ya grandes los quiquisques
    las patrullas entraban y salían con presos
    A Esteban lo montaron en el helicóptero
y al poco rato regresaron sin él …
    A Juan Hernández lo sacó la patrulla
una noche, y no regresó más
    Otra noche sacaron a Saturnino
y no lo volvimos a ver … a Chico González
    también se lo llevaron
    ésto casi cada noche
a la hora que cantan las cocorocas
gente que no conocimos también
    La Matilde abortó sentada
cuando toda una noche nos preguntaron por los guerrilleros

The Peasant Women from Cuá

Now I'll tell you about the cries from Cuá
cries of women like pangs of birth
María Venancia, 90 years old, deaf, half dead
    shouts at the soldiers, I haven't seen any boys
Amanda Aguilar, 50 years old
    with her daughters Petrona and Erlinda
      I haven't seen any boys
like pangs of birth
—Imprisoned three months straight in a mountain barrack—
Angela García, 25 years old and seven children,
    Cándida, 16 years old, suckles a baby girl
      very tiny and underfed
Many have heard these cries from Cuá
    wails from the homeland like pangs of birth
When she left jail, Estebana García, mother of four,
gave birth to another. She had to give up her children
    to a landowner. Emelinda Hernández, 16 years old,
      her cheeks shiny with tears,
    her braids wet from crying ...
They were captured in Tazua as they came from Waslala
    the cornfields in flower and the yucca full-grown
    the patrols came and went with prisoners
      They sent Esteban up in a helicopter
and soon after returned without him ...
      They carried off Juan Hernández
one night, and he never came back again
      Another night they took Saturnino
    and we never saw him again ... then they took
      Chico González
      it was the same almost every night
    at the hour the *cocorocas* sing
even people we didn't know
      Matilde aborted sitting down
when they questioned her all night long about the guerrillas

A la Cándida la llamó un guardia
vení lavame este pantalón
pero era para otra cosa
(Somoza sonreía en un retrato como un anuncio
de Alka-Seltzer)
Llegaron otros peores en un camión militar
A los tres días que salieron parió la Cándida
Esta es la historia de los gritos del Cuá
triste como el canto de las cocorocas
la historia que cuentan las campesinas del Cuá
    que cuentan llorando
como entreviendo tras la neblina de las lágrimas una cárcel
    y sobre ella un helicóptero
    "Nosotras no sabemos de ellos"
Pero sí han visto
           sus sueños son subversivos
barbudos, borrosos en la niebla
    rápidos
       pasando un arroyo
ocultos en la milpa
     apuntando
  (como pumas)
¡saliendo de los pajonales!
pijeando a los guardias
           viniendo al ranchito
   (sucios y gloriosos)
   la Cándida, la Amanda, la Emelinda
en sueños muchas noches
          —con sus mochilas—
   subiendo una montaña
     con cantos de dichoso-fui
la María Venancia de 90 años
    los ven de noche en sueños
       en extrañas montañas
muchas noches
    a los muchachos.

A guardsman called to Cándida
   come here and wash my pants
but he wanted something else
(Somoza smiled in a picture like
an Alka-Seltzer ad)
Worse ones came in an army truck
   Three days after they left Cándida gave birth
This is the story of the cries from Cuá
sad as the *cocoroca*'s song
the story that the peasant women from Cuá tell
   that they tell in tears
as though glimpsing a jail behind the mist of tears
   and above the jail a helicopter
   "We know nothing about them"
But they have seen
            their dreams are subversive
bearded, hazy in the mist
   quickly
      fording a stream
concealed in the cornfields
      taking aim
   (like pumas)
springing from the tall grass!
beating the guardsmen
            coming to the farm
   (dirty and triumphant)
   Cándida, Amanda, Emelinda
so often, at night, in dreams
            —with their knapsacks—
   climbing a mountain
      with happy-go-lucky songs
María Venancia, 90 years old,
   at night in their dreams they see the boys
      in strange mountains
so often at night in dreams
      they see the boys.
                  translated by Marc Zimmerman

Hartford Daylight

On the bus ride home
We pass through Hartford,
A landmark on the highway.
The dirty yellow G. Fox Building
Nudges the stream of traffic.
The Gold Building, the Capitol
Shoot sunlight across the city
Through the windows of the bus.

Today I heard on the radio
A worker who'd just been fired
Climbed one of the unfinished
Buildings in Hartford.
He had a rifle and ammunition.
The police talked him
Down, peacefully, before
His anger and frustration
Opened fire on pedestrians.

He's in jail now, or a
Madhouse—they serve
The same purpose

Those who fired him, who
Sold him the gun
Arrested him
Are walking free
Among the people in the street.

To A Cautious Poet

You can write poems
On venetian blinds,
Flash them on and
Off to the world.

Someday
The men with
The guns and butter
Will see you from the street,
Tramp up the stairs
To your room,
Strangle you with the
Cord of your caution.

Then they will praise you
As a tragic genius,
Your readers will admire
Your poems
While your body
Hangs
Behind the blinds.

Frente al balance, mañana

Y cuando se haga
el entusiasta recuento
de nuestro tiempo,
por los que todavía
no han nacido,
pero que se anuncian
con un rostro
más bondadoso,
saldremos gananciosos
los que más hemos
sufrido de él.

Y es que adelantarse
uno a su tiempo,
es sufrir mucho de él.

Pero es bello amar al mundo
con los ojos
de los que no han nacido
todavía.

Y espléndido,
saberse ya un victorioso,
cuando todo en torno a uno
es aún tan frío tan oscuro.

Before The Scales, Tomorrow

And when the enthusiastic
story of our time
is told,
for those
who are yet to be born
but announce themselves
with more generous face,
we will come out ahead
—those who have suffered most from it.

And that
being ahead of your time
means suffering much from it.

But it's beautiful to love the world
with eyes
that have not yet
been born.

And splendid
to know yourself victorious
when all around you
it's all still so cold,
so dark.

translated by Margaret Randall

Intelectuales apolíticos

Un día,
los intelectuales
apolíticos
de mi país
serán interrogados
por el hombre
sencillo
de nuestro pueblo.

Se les preguntará,
sobre lo que hicieron
cuando
la patria se apagaba
lentamente,
como una hoguera dulce,
pequeña y sola.

No serán interrogados
sobre sus trajes,
ni sobre sus largas
siestas
después de la merienda,
tampoco sobre sus estériles
combates con la nada,
ni sobre su ontológica
manera
de llegar a las monedas.
No sé les interrogará
sobre la mitología griega,
ni sobre el asco
que sintieron de sí,
cuando alguien, en su fondo,
se disponía a morir cobardemente.

Apolitical Intellectuals

One day
the apolitical
intellectuals
of my country
will be interrogated
by the simplest
of our people.

They will be asked
what they did
when their nation died out
slowly,
like a sweet fire,
small and alone.

No one will ask them
about their dress,
their long siestas
after lunch,
no one will want to know
about their sterile combats
with "the idea
of the nothing"
no one will care about
their higher financial learning.
They won't be questioned
on Greek mythology,
or regarding their self-disgust
when someone within them
begins to die
the coward's death.

Nada se les preguntará
sobre sus justificaciones
absurdas,
crecidas a la sombra
de una mentira rotunda.

Ese día vendrán
los hombres sencillos.
Los que nunca cupieron
en los libros y versos
de los intelectuales apolíticos,
pero que llegaban todos los días
a dejarles la leche y el pan,
los huevos y las tortillas,
los que les cosían la ropa,
los que les manejaban los carros,
les cuidaban sus perros y jardines,
y trabajaban para ellos,
                              y preguntarán,
"¿Qué hicistéis cuando los pobres
sufrían, y se quemaba en ellos,
gravemente, la ternura y la vida?"

Intelectuales apolíticos
de mi dulce país,
no podréis responder nada.

Os devorará un buitre de silencio
las entrañas.
Os roerá el alma
vuestra propia miseria.
Y callaréis,
                  avergonzados de vosotros.

They'll be asked nothing
about their absurd
justifications,
born in the shadow
of the total lie.

On that day
the simple men will come.
Those who had no place
in the books and poems
of the apolitical intellectuals,
but daily delivered
their bread and milk,
their tortillas and eggs,
those who mended their clothes,
those who drove their cars,
who cared for their dogs and gardens
and worked for them,
                          and they'll ask:
"What did you do when the poor
suffered, when tenderness
and life
burned out in them?"

Apolitical intellectuals
of my sweet country,
you will not be able to answer.

A vulture of silence
will eat your gut.
Your own misery
will pick at your soul.
And you will be mute
                          in your shame.

translated by Margaret Randall

Vámonos patria a caminar

1. Nuestra voz
2. Vámonos patria a caminar
3. Distante de tu rostro

1.

Para que los pasos no me lloren,
para que las palabras no me sangren:
canto.
Para tu rostro fronterizo del alma
que me ha nacido entre las manos:
canto.
Para decir que me has crecido clara
en los huesos más amargos de la voz:
canto.
Para que nadie diga: ¡tierra mía!,
con toda la decisión de la nostalgia:
canto.
Por lo que no debe morir, tu pueblo:
canto.

Me lanzo a caminar sobre mi voz para decirte:
tú, interrogación de frutas y mariposas silvestres,
no perderás el paso en los andamios de mi grito,
porque hay un maya alfarero en su corazón,
que bajo el mar, adentro de la estrella,
humeando en las raíces, palpitando mundo,
enreda tu nombre en mis palabras.
Canto tu nombre, alegre como un violín de surcos,
porque viene al encuentro de mi dolor humano.
Me busca del abrazo del mar hasta el abrazo del viento
para ordenarme que no tolere el crepúsculo en mi boca.

Let's Go, Country

1. Our voice
2. Let's go, country
3. Away from your face

1.

So that the path doesn't cry for me,
So I don't bleed through the words,
     I sing.
For your face the soul's frontier
born in my hands:
     I sing.
To say you have grown transparent
in the bitter bones of my voice:
     I sing.
So no one may say—my land!
with all the force of nostalgia
     I sing.
For those who must not die, your people,
     I sing.

Walking out over my voice I say:
you, interrogation of fruits and wild butterflies,
you will not lose your way in the scaffolding of my cry,
for there is a Mayan potter in your heart
who, under the sea, within the star,
smoking in root, palpitating world,
catches your name in my words.
I sing that name, joyful as the violin which is plough
:encounter of my human pain is still to come.
From the sea's arm to the arm of the wind they look for me
to break the tolerance of dusk in my mouth.

Me acompaña emocionado el sacrificio de ser hombre,
para que nunca baje al lugar donde nació la traición
del vil que ató su corazón a la tiniebla, negándote!

2.

Vámonos patria a caminar, yo te acompaño.

Yo bajaré los abismos que me digas.
Yo beberé tus cálices amargos.
Yo me quedaré ciego para que tengas ojos.
Yo me quedaré sin voz para que tú cantes.
Yo he de morir para que tú no mueras,
para que emerja tu rostro flameando al horizonte
de cada flor que nazca de mis huesos.

Tiene que ser así, indiscutiblemente.

Ya me cansé de llevar tus lágrimas conmigo.
Ahora quiero caminar contigo, relampagueante.
Acompañarte en tu jornada, porque soy un hombre
del pueblo, nacido en octubre para la faz del mundo.

Ay patria,
a los coroneles que orinan tus muros
tenemos que arrancarlos de raíces,
colgarlos en un árbol de rocío agudo,
violento de cóleras del pueblo.
Por ello pido que caminemos juntos. Siempre
con los campesinos agrarios
y los obreros sindicales,
con el que tenga un corazón para quererte.

Vámonos patria a caminar, yo te acompaño.

The sacrifice of being man accompanies me,
keeps me from going down to the place where treason's born,
where the fool chained his heart to shadow, denying you.

2.

Let's go, country, I will go with you.

I will descend the depths you claim for me.
I will drink of your bitter chalices.
I will remain blind that you may see.
I will remain voiceless that you may sing.
I will die that you may live,
so your flaming face appears
in every flower born of my bones.

That is the way it must be, unquestionably.

Now I am tired of carrying your tears with me.
Now I want to walk with you, in lightning step.
Go with you on your journey, because I am a man
of the people, born in October to confront the world.

Ay, country,
the colonels who piss on your walls
we must pull them out by the roots,
hang them from the tree of bitter dew,
violent with the anger of our people.
For this I say let us walk together, always
with the agrarian peasants
and the union workers,
with him who has a heart to know you.

Let's go, country, I will go with you.

3.

Pequeña patria mía, dulce tormenta,
un litoral de amor elevan mis pupilas
y la garganta se me llena de silvestre alegría
cuando digo patria, obrero, golondrina.
Es que tengo mil años de amanecer agonizando
y acostarme cadáver sobre tu nombre inmenso,
flotante sobre todos los alientos libertarios,
Guatemala, diciendo patria mía, pequeña campesina.

Ay, Guatemala,
cuando digo tu nombre retorno a la vida.
Me levanto del llanto a buscar tu sonrisa.
Subo las letras del alfabeto hasta la A
que desemboca al viento llena de alegría
y vuelvo a contemplarte como eres,
una raíz creciendo hacia la luz humana
con toda la presión del pueblo en las espaldas.
Desgraciados los traidores, madre patria, desgraciados.
¡Ellos conocerán la muerte de la muerte hasta la muerte!

¿Por qué nacieron hijos tan viles de madre cariñosa?

Así es la vida de los pueblos, amarga y dulce,
pero su lucha lo resuelve todo humanamente.
Por ello patria, van a nacerte madrugadas,
cuando el hombre revise luminosamente su pasado.
Por ello patria,
cuando digo tu nombre se rebela mi grito
y el viento se escapa de ser viento.
Los ríos se salen de su curso meditado
y vienen en manifestación para abrazarte.
Los mares conjugan en sus olas y horizontes

3.

My small country, sweet torment,
a bed of love lifts my pupils
and my throat fills wild with joy
when I say country, worker, *golondrina.*
A thousand years I have wakened in death
and laid my cadaver to sleep on your great name,
floating over all of freedom's breath,
Guatemala, saying, my country, little *campesina*

Ay, Guatemala,
saying your name I come back to life
I rise from the cry in search of your smile.
I raise the letters of the alphabet to A
where the wind flows out in gladness
and I return to contemplate you as you are,
a root growing towards the human light
with all the pressure of the people on your back.
Damned be the traitors,
> earth,
> mother,
>> damned!
They shall know the death of death until death!

From a loving mother, how are these vile sons born?

This is the life of the *pueblos*, bitter and sweet,
but her fight will put a human end to all.
For that, my country, dawns will be born of you,
when man revises luminously his past.
For that, my country,
when I say your name I reveal my cry
and the wind escapes its condition of wind.
The rivers leave their meditated course
and demonstrate, their arms about you.
The seas, on their waves and horizons,

tu nombre herido de palabras azules, limpio,
para llevarte hasta el grito acantilado del pueblo,
donde nadan los peces con aletas de auroras.

La lucha del hombre te redime en la vida.

Patria, pequeña, hombre y tierra y libertad
cargando la esperanza por los caminos del alba.
Eres la antigua madre del dolor y el sufrimiento.
La que marcha con un niño de maíz entre los brazos.
La que inventa huracanes de amor y cerezales
y se da redonda sobre la paz del mundo,
para que todos amen un poco de su nombre:
un pedazo brutal de sus montañas
o la heroica mano de sus hijos guerrilleros.

Pequeña patria, dulce tormenta mía,
canto ubicado en mi garganta
desde los siglos del maíz rebelde:
tengo mil años de llevar tu nombre
como un pequeño corazón futuro,
cuyas alas comienzan a abrirse a la mañana.

swear your name, wounded with blue words, clean,
to carry you to the people's piercing cry,
where fish swim with auroreal fins.

The fight of men redeems you in your life.

Country, small, man and land and liberty
carrying hope on morning paths.
You are the ancient mother of suffering and pain.
She who goes with a child of corn in her arms.
She who invents hurricanes of love and cherry shoots
and blossoms out over the peace of the world
so that all will love a little of your name:
a brutal piece of your mountains
or the heroic hand of your guerrilla sons.

Small country, my sweet torment,
song settling in my throat
from centuries of rebel corn:
for a thousand years I carry our name
like a tiny future heart,
whose wings begin to open tomorrow.

translated by Margaret Randall

Amelia, Mrs. Brooks of My Old Childhood

I

Amelia, Mrs. Brooks of my old childhood
I have come to you again.

I was job training in
New Jersey and a letter
came from someone
we did not know.

I asked my wife to
read it to me over
the telephone in
vague, irritated curiosity
and it was from someone
I had never heard of, your
Sister-in-law.

She admonished you loved me so much I
ought to be ashamed at my neglect of you, all these years.

II

"No-o, Amelyuh duzzent
live withus....No-o, Amelyuh's
across th'bridge t'Brewer, in a
nice nursing home....a nice! nursing home-n-her boys
live near by....No-o, Amelyuh don't know
y'cummin'....I wrote you. It was
my idea....I'll go telephone her now!
Y'gut a minute haven't you!? You'll go
see her!?"
....This one resents! She
can't put her finger on it but there's
something in the loose free easy
way I materialize at her door from
miles away within a week of receiving

a letter she just dashed off for
whatever reason....or was it
overwhelming for her to write...?

    She can't put it
into words but what it is is her kind
has lost control of me. I move in and out
and around them as I please and if I
please....I got away....she knows
I got away!

    From thin foundationless houses
plunked onto the earth, to the left a little from
Maine winters, like the old bow legged ladies inside,
sagging on teachers' pensions and dying in a rut
unable to even take a car trip because gas and motels
cost, stuck in the house for life, the only thing in
their lives now, dragging out to supermarket for
hamburger to make endless never changing meals of
meat cakes, peas, mashed potatoes cold in their pepper and salt
with the never melted butter clinging like a car that
has skidded on ice under snow to the side of a snow bank.

        III
Great lady of Sardines and
earth and blood of
Blueberryin' years, Clam Factory
years who brought up
children without help, a hopeless
drunk husband beating you in
his futility when the country was smashed.
Amelia, lady of poverty and no hope,
saint of this earth if ever there
is a saint and if not then you
are what was always instilled in us
as what a saint is, woman in the
retinas of God's eyes for your simple courage

and great accomplishment with no money
and from work that kills young, yet
you still live, Amelia, and here we are.

I came to you the day I
went into the army
    where sardines stuck
to your hands I came and said
goodbye in the fish smell.

You were beautiful, a
beautiful woman and
I yearned to say goodbye
to a mother.

You worked the Sardine Factories
    to feed your children.

No fish contributes
more to the human
race as Herring.
We sneak death again,
kill....take
herring from the sea our
boat circling, the Cannery
boats lifting the sardines
aboard into their holds
through hoses.

A Seine around
fish in moon black.

Draw string of net
pulled to close the
net bottom or the
fish sucked through hose....

To the Cannery as
soon as fish are
aboard, Herring
through a hose removing
their scales for imitation Pearl
essence on the Market Place
and Cosmetics.

IV
Amelia, the fish have less
chance than you had
except your death would
be more subtle, you died
from it, Amelia, died from exhausting
survival, your life wearing
out your life.

....no machine can pack sardines
like human hands, Amelia....

to feed your children.

Sitting in draughty cold
snipping off dead fish heads and tails
        with scissors.

    Yet death always a sneak, here
is food to eat but it will decompose
if we do not know that herring who have
just eaten must be allowed to swim it off until
they digest whatever was in them as you catch them....
or whatever they were eating avenges them as
bacteria planktonic form....

And once caught out of the fresh salt
protecting ocean if the fish are taken
distance of more than four hours they spoil,
Amelia....life is death all spoiled.

V

Amelia, did you go north
in the few years of the Winter Fisheries
to Eastport-Lubec, Maine, freezing
nets of two and one half inch mesh
sunk to the bottom in twenty
fathoms of water, fish catch
frozen solid on the market as "bloaters."

Amelia, sitting in frigid
cold icy sea water splashing
and wind finding you through
building cracks.

The cooked fish come down
conveyor belts for you to
pick up without breaking them
and put them into cans of
oil or mustard, fast!
You were fast all day
or out of work....

    to feed your children.

And to feed your children, bending in
Blueberry fields making your numb
fingers pick fast
to fill up pails quick
without bruising the blueberries
or you'd be out of work!

Vaccinium, that shrub
growing wild on barren uplands
of Maine bearing clustered, mild
sweet tasting fruit either blue
or purple black and coated with
greyish powder....Amelia you were

paid not by the time you
spent raking your bony hands blistered
slippery flesh but by the amount
you raked....There is no other way
to harvest blueberries other than to
bend over from the waist, tough back,
strong wrists, the strength
put in you by your children to
feed, to pull for, pull
pick through blueberry bushes
with a gentle rocking motion....

to feed your children.

Amelia, how could you love
Maine, the blood blue ocean,
the black green pines and
fresh yellow and green
dandelions with your nose
plowed in the earth or
in the stink of the
dead of the sea.

Although you were no whore
you were as exploited
and paid for piece work....

to feed your children.

VI
And into Clam Factories

to feed your children....

At night you'd take
hold of one of your hands with the other hand
and grip to squeeze out the pain of

Clam shell tiny cuts so you could sleep....to
be able to get up another morning to

feed your children.

And all you ever said anything
about was your sorrow at no time
or opportunity for education to be
accredited a nurse for the bed pans you carried
to feed your children....and assist the almost dying
whose saved lives never knew you were ignorant.

VII
In my lost mother boyhood
I stumbled over her kitchen cookies.

Now I am written
where she is in this world.

Her face is now under a spider web.
I have to look hard for
my memory to find it but
her voice is still
that inflection I remember.

She looks at me with
mixed emotions at best....if
I ever loved her at all then why
have thirty years gone without a

word from me, no note, never
a Christmas card....

Because she
is not the obligation my mother
would be....

I would not have you know, Amelia,
my years struggling to be my own me
and not what would please others who
would be under a head stone just
when I needed them, just as
our love affair was coming

And I called out

    "Here I am the way you wanted me"....but
they were not there.

          VIII
Amelia, Mrs. Brooks of my old childhood, I
have come to you again.

I was suddenly told where
to find you and I broke
New England until here
you and I are again, here
we are both of us in your
little apartment.

We both have died since
we've seen each other.

You speak to me now
and we both feel uncomfortable,
ours is a relationship of wish.

You tell me deaths and
I tell you deaths....
They almost killed us both
when they happened but telling
is embarrassing like what
are we talking about!

We have always lived
under the belief
that there is no help!

IX

....One of your sons, I remember him, Bob, I
served Mass with him on altars of
sour wine on early morning air and
bad breath smell from orifice emissions
in the middle of fervent prayers
and closed windows....Bob
tripped into an airplane propeller
instead of flying the plane
home for Thanksgiving.

Yet you tell this to me without
even a wince or remorse of
the anguish in your
voice or expression....

Because just going through
bringing him up
wore out your tears....long ago.

You lived through days you
never thought you'd see
the end of and yet
tomorrow was no relief.

And I do not react
either, death
will finally be my death.

It is strange to think you loved me,
the way you told your
Sister-in-law

"I just love that boy!"

You would like to love me I
was a boy with no mother and
you had no one either
and often thought of dying and
leaving your children
without a mother....

It makes you believe
you love me and
in your old years the
memory of little me running round
may make you believe
you love me.

X

Now in this midnight of
my lost mother boyhood we may
never see each other again.

A letter appeared telling me
where you were and since I
found myself still alive I
came to you once more....

The sea is in
your voice and my life is
etched in the lines of your face.

If a woman like you wants to
think she loves me, take me
again in your heart in my old childhood.
For soon earth will cover us.

Para un mejor amor

"El sexo es una categoría política."—Kate Millet

Nadie discute que el sexo
es una categoría en el mundo de la pareja:
de ahí la ternura y sus ramas salvajes.

Nadie discute que el sexo
es una categoría familiar:
de ahí los hijos,
las noches en común
y los días divididos
(él, buscando el pan en la calle,
en las oficinas o en las fábricas;
ella, en la retaguardia de los oficios domésticos,
en la estrategia y la táctica de la cocina
que permitan sobrevivir en la batalla común
siquiera hasta el fin del mes).

Nadie discute que el sexo
es una categoría económica:
basta mencionar la prostitución,
las modas,
las secciones de los diarios que sólo son para ella
o sólo son para él.

Donde empiezan los líos
es a partir de que una mujer dice
que el sexo es una categoría política.

Porque cuando una mujer dice
que el sexo es una categoría política
puede comenzar a dejar de ser mujer en sí

Toward A Better Love

"Sex is a political condition."—Kate Millet

No one disputes that sex
is a condition in the world of the couple:
from there, tenderness and its wild branches.

No one disputes that sex
is a domestic condition:
from there, kids,
nights in common
and days divided
(he, looking for bread in the street,
in offices or factories;
she, in the rear-guard of domestic functions,
in the strategy and tactic of the kitchen
that allows survival in a common struggle
at least to the end of the month).

No one disputes that sex
is an economic condition:
it's enough to mention prostitution,
fashion,
the sections in the dailies that are only for her
or only for him.

Where the hassles begin
is when a woman says
sex is a political condition.

Because when a woman says
sex is a political condition
she can begin to stop being just a woman in herself

para convertirse en mujer para sí,
constituir a la mujer en mujer
a partir de su humanidad
y no de su sexo,
saber que el desodorante mágico con sabor a limón
y jabón que acaricia voluptuosamente su piel
son fabricados por la misma empresa que fabrica el napalm
saber que las labores propias del hogar
son las labores propias de la clase social a que pertenece ese hogar,
que la diferencia de sexos
brilla mucho mejor en la profunda noche amorosa
cuando se conocen todos esos secretos
que nos mantenían enmascarados y ajenos.

in order to become a woman for herself,
establishing the woman in woman
from the basis of her humanity
and not of her sex,
knowing that the magic deodorant with a hint of lemon
and soap that voluptuously caresses her skin
are made by the same manufacturer that makes napalm
knowing the labors of the home themselves
are labors of a social class to which that home belongs,
that the difference between the sexes
burns much better in the loving depth of night
when all those secrets that kept us
masked and alien are revealed.

translated by Jack Hirschman

Como tú

Yo, como tú,
amo el amor, la vida, el dulce encanto
de las cosas, el paisaje
celeste de los días de enero.

También mi sangre bulle
y río por los ojos
que han conocido el brote de las lágrimas.

Creo que el mundo es bello,
que la poesía es como el pan, de todos.

Y que mis venas no terminan en mí
sino en la sangre unánime
de los que luchan por la vida,
el amor,
las cosas,
el paisaje y el pan,
la poesía de todos.

Like You

Like you I
love love, life, the sweet smell
of things, the sky-blue
landscape of January days.

And my blood boils up
and I laugh through eyes
that have known the buds of tears.

I believe the world is beautiful
and that poetry, like bread, is for everyone.

And that my veins don't end in me
but in the unanimous blood
of those who struggle for life,
love,
little things,
landscape and bread,
the poetry of everyone.

translated by Jack Hirschman

Sobre el negocio bíblico

Dice la Biblia
que Cristo multiplicó para el pueblo
el pan y los peces.

Si lo hizo, hizo bien,
y eso lo hace más grande que un gran general
que ganara mil batallas donde murieron millones de pobres.

Pero en la actualidad los norteamericanos
para evitar que el pan y los peces se multipliquen
y todo el mundo soporte con resignación
el hambre multiplicada que es parte del gran negocio,
multiplican la producción de Biblias
en todos los idiomas que hablamos los pobres
y nos las envían en manos de jóvenes rubios
que han sido minuciosamente adiestrados por sus generales.

On Biblical Business

The Bible says
Christ multiplied bread
and fish for the people.

If that's so, he did well
and that makes him greater than a great general
who wins a thousand battles in which millions of poor people die.

But at present the North Americans,
to see that bread and fish don't multiply
and that everyone suffers in resignation
the multiplied hunger that's part of big business,
step up production of Bibles
in all the dialects we poor speak
and ship them to us in the hands of blond young men
who've been thoroughly trained by their generals.

translated by Jack Hirschman

La certeza

(Sobre una idea de V. G.)

Después de cuatro horas de tortura, el Apache y los otros dos cuilios le echaron un balde de agua al reo para despertarlo y le dijeron: "Manda a decir el Coronel que te va a dar un chance de salvar la vida. Si adivinas quién de nosotros tiene un ojo de vidrio, te dejaremos de torturar." Después de pasear su mirada sobre los rostros de sus verdugos, el reo señaló a uno de ellos: "El suyo. Su ojo derecho es de vidrio."

Y los cuilios asombrados dijeron: "Te salvaste! pero ¿cómo has podido adivinarlo? Todos tus cheros fallaron, porque el ojo es americano, es decir, perfecto." "Muy sencillo"—dijo el reo, sintiendo que le venía otra vez el desmayo—"fue el único ojo que no me miró con odio."

Desde luego, lo siguieron torturando.

The Certainty

(On an idea of V.G.)

After four hours of torture, the Apache and the other two cops threw a bucket of water at the prisoner to wake him up and said: "The Colonel has ordered us to tell you you're to be given a chance to save your skin. If you guess which of us has a glass eye, you'll be spared torture." After passing his gaze over the faces of his executioners, the prisoner pointed to one of them: "His. His right eye is glass."

And the astonished cops said, "You're saved! But how did you guess? All your buddies missed because the eye is American, that is, perfect." "Very simple," said the prisoner, feeling he was going to faint again, "it was the only eye that looked at me without hatred."

Of course they continued torturing him.

translated by Jack Hirschman

Đất đỏ–nước xanh

Bom đào đất đỏ, đỏ au
chói chang trưa nắng một màu lửa nung

Phễu bom sâu hóa giếng hồng
đất tuôn lặng lẽ một dòng nước xanh

Quê mình đó phải không anh?
Đau thương mấy vẫn ngọt lành bên trong.

Miền Tây Quảng Bình 1971

Red Earth–Blue Water

Bombs plowed into the red earth, berry red.
Scorching sunlight burned the noon air like kiln fire.

Bomb-raked funnels turned into rose-water wells,
A noiseless stream of blue water gushing up.

That's our country, isn't it, friend?
The maddening agony, the honey comes from within.

Western Quang Binh, 1971

translated by Kevin Bowen and Nguyen Ba Chung

Buổi Sang Sau Chiến Tranh

Mịn làm sao mát làm sao
bụi sương thôi cũng ngọt ngào trên môi

Sương giăng lụt cả đất trời
giữa bồng bềnh trắng tôi bơi tôi trườn

Con đường chìm nổi trong sương
thực hư như thể con đường trong mơ

Chờ em...lẳng lặng...tôi chờ
lập lòe hoa gạo lờ mờ bóng cây

Hố bom sâu hoắm nơi này
sương mong mỏng lấp đã dày từ đêm

Loeo khoeo cột điện cột đèn
lô nhô huyền ảo đẹp lên lạ kỳ

Dịu dàng từng bước em đi
nhẹ nhàng như chả có gì lớn lao...

Hà Nội 1975

The Morning After the War Was Over

So smooth, fragile, so fresh and sweet,
specks of moisture, dust, cool on the lip.

The entire universe dissolved in a blanket of mist,
I ride and swim the waves of white.

Roads appear, disappear in haze,
reality, illusion, a dream.

I wait...in silence...for you,
tree shadows blur, kapok flowers flicker and wave.

A bomb driven deep in earth, a white mist hovering
imperceptibly over its crater since evening.

Lampposts thin as reeds in the street,
spiked shadows like children's magic shows.

You move softly step by step,
easily, as if it were nothing at all...

Hanoi, 1975

translated by Kevin Bowen and Nguyen Ba Chung

Đò Lèn

thưở nhỏ tôi ra cống Na câu cá
níu váy bà đi chợ Bình Lâm
bắt chim sẻ ở vành tai tượng phật
và đôi khi ăn trộm nhãn chùa Trần

thưở nhỏ tôi lên chơi đền Cây Thị
chân đất đi xem lễ đền Sòng
mùi huệ trắng quyện khói trầm thơm lắm
điệu hát văn lảo đảo bóng cô đồng

tôi đâu biết bà tôi cơ cực thế
bà mò cua xúc tép ở đồng Quan
bà đi gánh chè xanh Ba Trại
Quán Cháo, Đồng Giao thập thững những đêm hàn

tôi trong suốt giữa hai bờ hư—thực
giữa bà tôi và tiên phật, thánh thần
cái năm đói củ dong riềng luộc sượng
cứ nghe thơm mùi huệ trắng hương trầm

bom Mỹ dội—nhà bà tôi bay mất
đền Sòng bay, bay tuốt cả chùa chiền
thánh với phật rủ nhau đi đâu hết
bà tôi đi bán trứng ở ga Lèn

tôi đi lính...lâu không về quê ngoại
dòng sông xưa vẫn bên lở bên bồi
khi tôi biết thương bà thì đã muộn
bà chỉ còn là một nấm cỏ thôi!

Quê ngoại 9.1983

Do Len

When I was a boy I spent my days fishing at the Na Brook
or holding my grandmother's skirt in Binh Lam market
or catching sparrows on the great Buddha's ears
or stealing longans from the Tran Pagoda.

At night I played barefoot at the Cay Thi shrine
joined the crowds at the Song temple festival,
the white lilies smelled sweeter in the incense smoke,
the medium staggering in pace with the old songs.

I didn't think of her hard life then: how my grandmother
scooped prawns and groped for crabs in the Quan field,
how she wobbled with those baskets of green beans
                                    on her shoulders
going to Ba Trai, Quan Chao, Dong Giao, cold freezing nights.

I lived between the banks of truth and untruth,
between my grandmother and angels, buddhas and gods.
I remember the year of famine and the *dong* roughly cooked,
did I smell the fragrance of incense and white lilies then?

But soon the bombs began falling. My grandmother's house
                                    blew away,
the Song temple blew away, the pagoda blew away,
the gods and buddhas left together,
my grandmother sold eggs at the Len train stop.

I joined the army...traveled far from my village many years,
the old river with one bank crumbling, one bank built up.
I found my love for my grandmother too late,
a grassy mound all that was left.

Mother's village, 9/1983

translated by Kevin Bowen and Nguyen Ba Chung

La tumba de Buenaventura Roig

for my great-grandfather, died 1941

Buenaventura Roig,
once peasants in the thousands
streamed down hillsides
to witness the great eclipse
of your funeral.
Now your bones have drifted
with the tide of steep grass,
sunken in the chaos of weeds
bent and suffering
like canecutters in the sun.
The drunken caretaker
cannot find the grave,
squinting at your name,
spitting as he stumbles
between the white Christs
with hands raised
sowing their field
of white crosses.

Buenaventura Roig,
in Utuado you built the stone bridge
crushed years later by a river
raving like a forgotten god;
here sweat streaked your face
with the soil of coffee,
the ground where your nephew slept
while rain ruined the family crop,
and his blood flowered like flamboyán
on the white suit of his suicide.

La tumba de Buenaventura Roig

para mi bisabuelo, fallecido en 1941

Buenaventura Roig,
una vez miles de peones
bajaron de las colinas como una cascada
para presenciar el gran eclipse
de tu entierro.
Ahora tus huesos se han ido a la deriva
con la corriente de yerbas brujas empinadas,
hundidos en el caos de malezas
agachadas y sufrientes
como macheteros bajo el sol.
El celador borracho
no halla la tumba,
mirando bizco en búsqueda de tu nombre,
escupiendo al tropezarse
entre Cristos blancos
con manos levantadas
sembrando su campo
de cruces blancas.

Buenaventura Roig,
en Utuado levantaste
el puente de piedra
aplastado años después por un río
desvariado como un dios olvidado;
aquí el sudor rayó tu cara
con tierra cafetalera,
el suelo donde durmió tu sobrino
mientras las lluvias arruinaban la cosecha de la familia,
y la sangre floreció como el flamboyán
en el traje blanco de su suicidio.

Buenaventura Roig,
in the town plaza where you were mayor,
where there once was a bench
with the family name,
you shouted subversion
against occupation armies and sugarcane-patrones
to the jíbaros who swayed
in their bristling dry thicket of straw hats,
who knew bundles and sacks
loaded on the fly-bitten beast
of a man's back.

Buenaventura Roig,
not enough money for a white Christ,
lost now even to the oldest gravedigger,
the one with an English name
descended from the pirates of the coast,
who grabs for a shirt-pocket cigarette
as he remembers your funeral,
a caravan trailing in the distance
of the many years
that cracked the skin around his eyes.

Buenaventura Roig,
we are small among mountains,
and we listen for your voice
in the peasant chorus of five centuries,
waiting for the cloudburst of wild sacred song,
pouring over the crypt-wreckage of graveyard,
over the plaza and the church
where the statue of San Miguel
still chokes the devil with a chain.

Buenaventura Roig,
en la plaza del pueblo del que fuiste alcalde,
donde alguna vez había una banca marcada
con el apellido de la familia,
gritaste subversión
contra ejércitos de ocupación y los patrones de la caña
a los jíbaros que se mecían
entre su seca maleza híspida de pavas,
que bien sabían de bultos y bolsas
cargadas sobre la bestia
de una espalda humana
hostigada por moscas.

Buenaventura Roig,
demasiado poco dinero para un Cristo blanco,
perdido ahora hasta para el sepulturero más anciano,
el de apellido inglés
de ascendencia pirata costeña,
que agarra un cigarillo del bolsillo de su camisa
al recordar tu entierro,
una caravana desvaneciéndose en la distancia
de tantos años
que rajaron la piel alrededor de sus ojos.

Buenaventura Roig,
somos pequeños entre montañas,
y buscamos escuchar tu voz
entre el coro campesino de cinco siglos,
esperando el nubarrón de cantos sagrados salvajes,
derramándose sobre los pabellones arruinados del camposanto,
sobre la plaza y la iglesia
donde la estatua de San Miguel
todavía estrangula al diablo con una cadena.

translated by Camilo Pérez-Bustillo & Martín Espada

Federico's Ghost

The story is
that whole families of fruitpickers
still crept between the furrows
of the field at dusk,
when for reasons of whiskey or whatever
the cropduster plane sprayed anyway,
floating a pesticide drizzle
over the pickers
who thrashed like dark birds
in a glistening white net,
except for Federico,
a skinny boy who stood apart
in his own green row,
and, knowing the pilot
would not understand in Spanish
that he was the son of a whore,
instead jerked his arm
and thrust an obscene finger.

The pilot understood.
He circled the plane and sprayed again,
watching a fine gauze of poison
drift over the brown bodies
that cowered and scurried on the ground,
and aiming for Federico,
leaving the skin beneath his shirt
wet and blistered,
but still pumping his finger at the sky.

After Federico died,
rumors at the labor camp
told of tomatoes picked and smashed at night,
growers muttering of vandal children

El fantasma de Federico

Cuentan que
familias enteras de peones
aún se arrastraban entre los surcos
de los campos al anochecer,
cuando a raíz de whiskey o lo que sea
el avión regador roció de todas maneras,
dejando flotar una llovizna pesticida
sobre los que piscaban,
retorciéndose como pájaros oscuros
en una blanca red reluciente,
todos menos Federico,
un flaco joven de pie aparte
en su propio surco verde,
que a sabiendas de que el piloto
no comprendería en español
lo que era un hijo de puta,
sacudió su brazo
y lo embistió con un dedazo obsceno.

El piloto comprendió.
Hizo girar el avión y regó de nuevo,
mirando la fina gasa de veneno
esparcirse por encima de los cuerpos morenos
que se refugiaron y arrastraron por el suelo,
y haciéndole blanco a Federico,
dejándole la piel mojada y ampollada
por debajo de la camisa,
aún embistiendo su dedo hacia el cielo.

Después de que murió Federico,
los chismes en el campamento de trabajo
hablaban de tomates piscados y aplastados de noche,
terratenientes murmullando de niños vándalos

or communists in camp,
first threatening to call Immigration,
then promising every Sunday off
if only the smashing of tomatoes would stop.

Still tomatoes were picked and squashed
in the dark,
and the old women in camp
said it was Federico,
laboring after sundown
to cool the burns on his arms,
flinging tomatoes
at the cropduster
that hummed like a mosquito
lost in his ear,
and kept his soul awake.

o comunistas infiltrados,
primero amenazando con llamar a la Migra,
después prometiendo domingos sin trabajo
a cambio de que dejaran de machacar los tomates.

Pero los tomates seguían siendo piscados y aplastados
en la oscuridad,
y las ancianas del campamento
decían que era Federico,
trabajando después del anochecer
para calmar las quemaduras en sus brazos,
lanzándole tomates
al avión regador
que zumbaba como un mosquito
perdido en su oído,
manteniendo su alma despierta.

translated by Camilo Pérez-Bustillo & Martín Espada

Jorge the Church Janitor Finally Quits

Cambridge, Massachusetts, 1989

No one asks
where I am from,
I must be
from the country of janitors,
I have always mopped this floor.
Honduras, you are a squatter's camp
outside the city
of their understanding.

No one can speak
my name,
I host the fiesta
of the bathroom,
stirring the toilet
like a punchbowl.
The Spanish music of my name
is lost
when the guests complain
about toilet paper.

What they say
must be true:
I am smart,
but I have a bad attitude.

No one knows
that I quit tonight,
maybe the mop
will push on without me,

Por fin renuncia Jorge el conserje de la iglesia

Cambridge, Massachusetts, 1989

Nadie me pregunta
de dónde soy,
tendré que ser
de la patria de los conserjes,
siempre he trapeado este piso.
Honduras, eres un campamento de desamparados
afuera de la ciudad
de su comprensión.

Nadie puede decir
mi nombre,
yo soy el amenizador
de la fiesta en el baño,
meneando el agua en el inodoro
como si fuera una ponchera.
La música española de mi nombre
se pierde
cuando los invitados se quejan
del papel higiénico.

Será verdad
lo que dicen:
soy listo,
pero tengo una mala actitud.

Nadie sabe
que esta noche renuncié al puesto,
quizá el trapero
seguirá adelante sin mí,

sniffing along the floor
like a crazy squid
with stringy gray tentacles.
They will call it Jorge.

husmeando el piso
como un calamar enloquecido
con fibrosos tentáculos grises.
Lo llamarán Jorge.

translated by Camilo Pérez-Bustillo & Martín Espada

The Scientist

He was a refugee from a continent
        strewn with limbs.
He was at home with infinity
        and with numbers,
A true believer in peace.

When the great equation flashed
        like a missile
Across his brain, he stood
        as on a nova,
Holding the future of all creatures
        in fee simple.

Did he in that instant see the terror
        in mankind,
Or know he was Genghis Khan
        incarnate
Who could not turn back,
        or would not,
From that slaughter on the plain?

He was a good man,
Not the first
Or last
To let angels die.

Neighborhood Watch

They are waiting for the night visitor
Who comes unseen through the iron grid.
They are praying for the family jewels
Or the sacred white jaguar
Locked in its cave in the dark.

Meanwhile the dehydrated old man
Is dying of loneliness in his house,
The widow next door strangles a cat
      for the same reason,
The husband and wife in the doomed
      bungalow
Are on the crumbling edge of mayhem.

A country in love with itself
Cannot regurgitate its worldly goods
      in time.
It awaits the millennium in the museum
Where the stuffed eagle stares
      with glassy eyes
Into the lean and ghostly past.

The Sea Of Tranquility

is on the moon where no one needs it,
A boundless meadow of dust
Made by a meteor in some dark age
    of heaven.
Meanwhile, the very words quiet us
    like sleep.

The name of that sea is required
    on earth
To untangle the nerves in the streets
    of the city,
To reduce the cries in the beds
    of the closed ward,
To open a vast blue placid eye
    upon the fields of blood.

We have to invent a sea of tranquility
    in the heartland,
A calm world in a curve of trees,
    spacious, silent,
Cooling the fevers with a landscape
    of hope and repose.

Forever in the depths of the black hole
    of time
Is an idea that seeks to emerge
    in the light.
We await the second coming: the birth
    of the great sea.

At Saint Anthony's

I almost ran up to her to say,
"Hey Jazzy, you coming to workshop today?"
but saw her head
turned towards the wall
of St. Anthony's
like a broken doll's head
and her exhausted hungry eyes;
and I remembered:
being poor
takes twice
the effort.

For Pablo Neruda

This day
like no other
will soon pass.

But now
the glamorous sea
flaunts her diamond surfaced brilliance.

The sun traverses the sky awakening other
worlds of sleepers

The moon will climb
its silken laddered perch
and embrace us in its
milky attraction
and a little sadness.

Soon, this day
like no other
will be gone.

Deep in the night
I feel the kiss of the sun
the murmured seduction of the
wind
the tingling feeling of sand on skin.

The results of this day unlike the morrow
or the morrow, or the morrow.

This day when we are alive.

Among The Yurok

Among the California Yurok
all the great doctors were women.
The last, Fanny Flounder (1870-1945),
suspended her redwood house on a bluff
over the mouth of the Klamath River,
half in sky, half in ocean.
She sees the earth weightless,
tipping into the sea,
no Yurok feet to hold it firm.
She weaves baskets tall as men to weight
the earth, to balance earth, air, and water.
As a girl, after summers
of dancing for power,
she danced to the horizon and sucked blood.
She learned to swallow pains,
to cast pain out, fluttering,
to weave a dance with pain in her hand.
> The pain is her gift.
> The dance is her gift.
> The cure is her gift.
She lives on the horizon, singing
to suck out blood:
> "When the sky moves up and down
> you are traveling in air."

from *Love After the Riots*

9:40pm

Hear the footsteps. The flower shriek in my hand
sways the flood, down the stairs.
We talk about the red sirens and wonder
about our tongues. I wonder.
In this apartment everything is possible.
Motorcycle leather cops
turn the corner towards the piers.

Still, her glasses
make her look courteous and severe.
Lay down and smile. Move the cartoon
arms up with abandon, again. We embrace
against the boards.

Rodney King's handsome face
flashes through the curtain, it flashes
across my forehead.

3:45am

She asks them what are you doing
to put the fires out?
I know she is asking me.

Praying too.

She says
something like this:
A torch, a line of torches, men
in plumber uniforms, in laundry jackets,

a blackened sky with a little boy & girl rustling
their feet in the silk. A vigil. Floating pillows
crushed bed posts, open night-cream jars.

Human Interlude

for Terry Garvin

She was standing against
   the wall near
the Tevere Hotel holding
   a plastic cup
as it began to rain.

I dug for a coin, walked
   up to her
and dropped it in.
   It fell to the bottom
of an orange drink.

I blushed, looked into her
   ravaged eyes and skin
      and hair prematurely
greying, and said
I was sorry, I'd thought

she needed some bread.
   "I do," she said
and smiled, "I was
   just having a little
      drink."

And we stood there
   laughing together
as we watched the raindrops fall
   on the orange lake
above the drowning money.

In Memoriam
Ray Thompson (1943-1990)

Of the streets,
of begging hands and windblown cardboard,
of flophouse doorways or the lot behind the autobody shop,
of evictions from one downpour to another
and the trembling coffee,
the burning corner can,
the scavenged alleys,
the scratched and ravaged graffiti,
the transient handbills
and collectives of alone,

he was a poet
who wrote the deep lines the rotting weather
of this system cuts into human faces,
who saw in the cracks and the fissures
endurance birthing flashes of a radiant
lava-whirl of erupting rage,
and how hungry hunger is for it!
how widespread homelessness is for it!
how fertile futility is for it!
in this land where every living being or thing
is up for grabs or sale,
how headlong suffering is for it!

Earth, be mended
in the tears
of your seams, O ragged Earth,
be healed in your desire
for his body
through these tears. Mix him
with the thunders you've stored,

and with the rains,
the suns, the lightningcracks
and the strokes of your loving zodiac
wrap him home, wound in his friends'
never-ending memory of his ascendings.

Undone Day

You think I like being a dime bag in a doorway?
Living in a bottle in an alley?
Macho with the needlework of biceps?
You think I want this sweatshop of libernada?
Nowhere is the place where ...
Immigrant from my own ...
If I feel all the way to you, país,
¡Qué triste!

How small they want us
all, who never were
tall to begin with,

smaller than small—measly,
measlier than measly—crushed,
though our language can
hope so deeply and weep so full of stars.

Pobrecito Ricardo covered with bugs
where we found him,
a fleabag in a fleabag hotel,
how you say in spanish
even his death had to clear out
by seven in the morning.

Undone day
light in the eyes of the 18
as the boxcar door slammed shut
and night with fingernails
screaming against steel
the graffiti of
dying gasps on the inside of
the oven.

Undone day
of migrant wanderers pickpicking
pickpicking berries and crumbs
filling pittance baskets
under tortillas of smog.

Undone day
rubiado remembering how somewhere
tasted with all five senses,
how it was poor but like a leaflet
or a child in another's eyes.

Not this always Goliath of money towering
and myself a gob of saliva crazy for a sling,
not this broken fanta of youthful dignity,
not these disappeared *que paso*s.

Undone day
desperado waiting for
my moan to reach the end of its decibel,
a hand to lift my earthquake
to the level of foundation,
a hope to organize my debris
into more than this little cell
going from one key to another
in search of the outside of in.

Haiti

One day in the future these sounds are seeds of,
there will be a moment when not even the monkeys chirp in the
trees,
when burros will hold their brays,
when the coconut-milky clouds will not stir in the sky,
when the thatchwork of huts will not be gossiping
and there is no breeze or sweat between your body and your rags.
One day when that moment lived for years, for centuries, is here
and everything is still
like death
or zombie bread holding its breath,
a drum will begin sounding
and then another and another, multiplying,
and the voices of the simidors will be heard in every field.
And the backs,
those backs with everything written on them,
which have bent like nails hammered into the wooden cross
of the land for ages,
will plunge their arms into the ground
and pull out the weapons they've planted.
For the drums aren't an invitation to a voodoo ceremony.
The voices of the simidors are singing another song.
The lambis are growling lions of Africa.
And it isn't the cranium of a horse hung on the wooden cross
braided with limes;
it isn't a wooden cross at all that's planted in the good earth
of new Haiti.

On the night of that day the taste of a mango will be
a rapturous fireworks bursting and dying into
the ecstasy of the simple truth in our mouths.
Our acres will sleep with their arms round each other.

The child freed from terror and death will bound with the boundless, and the maize amaze the sky upon waking for as long as humanity is.

This Neruda Earth

Sitting against a treetrunk in Dolores Park
amid the Chilean solidarity gathering,
my eyes beheld three tiny daisies
in the grass, their little pollen hearts
attacked by flies. Nearby, yellowjackets
were flying over a jungle of blades
of grass and brilliantly green-backed
horseflies were making merry on
a flute of dogshit. I had lowered
my eyes from the speeches, and even
the People's Tribune was stacked at
my side. So much movement
in nature. A butterfly alighted on
the front page and walked along
the headline as if reading it. The
flies went on eating the hearts out.
The horseflies were absolutely drunken
on the excrement. The yellowjackets
were strafing and landing and
taking off again. It was the guerrilla
war, it was *mir*, it was peace. So much
movement, so much space in an inch. This
Neruda earth.

Desconcierto

A mis
Viejos
Maestros
De marxismo
No los puedo
Entender:
Unos están
En la cárcel
Otros están
En el
Poder

Confusion

As for
my old
teachers
of Marxism
I don't
understand them:
Some are
in prison
others are
in power.

translated by Jim Normington

Despliegue de asombros ante un dios

Lo primero es el cielo. Después viene
el espléndido dios que todo lo atruena
con su nariz agujereada y sus miembros
comidos por el hambre de siglos.

El dios vivo y marcado, ungido
con cenizas y lágrimas en cada poro.
El dios traído a un templo a través de otros
templos y otras catedrales y otros misterios.

El dios puesto de pie, venerado,
herido de dolor y de miseria.

Oh dios de cielos y caminos, dios
de agua y furor, dios maldito de misericordia,
devóranos con tu boca sin labios
y tu dura palabra de serpientes heladas.

Oh sordo, ciego y luminoso dios,
enciende alguna vez el rostro del pueblo,
de este bosque sin dueño, propiedad
de todos y de nadie. Patria de espejos
y mediodías, patria embriagada de muerte.

Húndela, inúndela, oh dios sacado
del secreto, dios que miró abrirse
vientres mestizos y padeció la primera herradura.

Unfurling Of Amazements Before God

The first thing is the sky. After that comes
the magnificent god who stuns everybody
with his perforated nose and his limbs
eaten by the hunger of centuries.

The living and marked god,
anointed with ashes and tears in every pore.
The ragged god in a temple across from other temples
and other cathedrals and other mysteries.

The god standing upright, venerated,
wounded by pain and poverty.

Oh god of skies and roads, god
of water and passion, god cursed by forgiveness,
devour us with your lipless mouth
and your harsh words made of frozen snakes.

Oh deaf, blind, luminous god,
light up the face of the nation
in this forest without a landlord,
the property of everybody and nobody. Country of mirrors
and 12 o'clock noons, country drunk on death.

Destroy it, flood it out, oh god pulled loose
from the secret, god who watched mestizo guts open
and who suffered the first horseshoe.

translated by Jim Normington

De repente

¿Qué les pasa a las calles traga-gentes
de repente?
Calles antropófagas se han vuelto
de repente
estas vulgares, rectas calles
afeitadas cada hora
con la crema azul del smog de cada día.
De repente
son calles espadachines de la muerte,
largos caminos directos a las celdas;
nadie sabe si sabe su destino.
De repente
sólo la calle sabe
cuantos guardias aguardan en la esquina,
cuantos policías disfrazados
acechan al que sale de su casa.
De repente
se han vuelto cómplices del crimen.
De repente
se han hecho espías y asesinas.
De repente
se comen a la gente con zapatos,
con portadocumentos,
con la fotografía de la novia;
todo desaparece en la garganta
de este nuevo verdugo.
De repente,
estas mismas calles que pasean
a mamás con bebés,
a dulces
mujeres embarazadas,
estan tejiendo redes traicioneras

All of a Sudden

What is it with these people-swallowing streets
all of a sudden?
They've become cannibal streets
all of a sudden
these straight, commonplace streets
groomed every hour
with the blue cream of an everyday smog.
All of a sudden
the streets at either hand are goons of death,
long ways direct to jail cells.
No one knows if he knows his destination
is his destiny.
All of a sudden
only the street knows
how many guards wait at the corner,
how many policemen in disguise
watch for the one who leaves his house.
All of a sudden
they've become accomplices in crime.
All of a sudden
they've become spies and assassins.
All of a sudden
they eat people with shoes
with i.d. cards
with a snapshot of the sweetheart,
it all disappears down the throat
of this new executioner.
All of a sudden
these same streets, strolling with
mothers with babies,
sweet
pregnant women—
are knitting treacherous webs

y apostando un agente en cada esquina.
De repente
estas calles urbanas,
cotidianas,
se ponen a aullar
y de la niebla
surgen las gargantas de los lobos.
De repente
un certero golpe solapado
y se tragan al muchacho,
a la muchacha,
por 15 días,
       por un mes,
             por siempre.

and posting an agent at each corner.
All of a sudden
these urbane streets,
everyday-like,
start howling
and from the fog
the throats of wolves come out.
All of a sudden
a sly perfect coup
and they swallow the boy,
the girl,
for 15 days,
    for a month,
        for ever

translated by
Maria A. Proser, Arlene Scully & James Scully

Refranes   Chile, 1973 en adelante

1) Otra cosa es con metralla
2) En boca cerrada no entran balas
3) En casa del obrero cuchillo y bala
4) No ver, no oir, no hablar
5) La momia aunque se vista de obrera momia se queda
6) Cuando el momio suena, mierda lleva
7) Una mano delata la otra y las dos delatan la cara
8) Uno solo bien se calla, pero dos se callan mejor
9) Camarón que se duerme se lo llevan a Tres Alamos
10) Más vale un avión en el suelo que cien volando
11) Cría soldados y te matarán los hijos
12) Cuando una celda se cierra doscientas se abren
13) Por la boca muere usted
14) A Mercedes regalado no se le mira el diente

Los refranes originales:
1) Otra cosa es con guitarra
2) En boca cerrada no entran moscas
3) En casa del herrero cuchillo de palo
4) No ver, no oir, no hablar
5) La mona aunque se vista de seda, mona se queda
6) Cuando el río suena, piedras lleva
7) Una mano lava la otra y las dos lavan la cara
8) Buey solo bien se lame, pero dos se lamen mejor
9) Camarón que se duerme, se lo lleva la corriente
10) Más vale un pájaro en la mano que cien volando
11) Cría cuervos y te sacarán los ojos
12) Cuando una puerta se cierra doscientas se abren
13) Por la boca muere el pez
14) A caballo regalado no se le mira el diente

Nota:
momio: gente de derecha
Tres Alamos: una prisión
Mercedes: Mercedes Benz, muy de moda actualmente entre los
    altos grados de las FF. AA.

Proverbs   Chile, 1973 on

1) It's altogether something else with shrapnel
2) In closed mouth no bullets enter
3) In the house of the worker: knife & bullet
4) See not, hear not, speak not
5) The mummy, though dressed as a worker, is a mummy still
6) When the mummy sounds off, the shit carries
7) One hand betrays the other & both betray the face
8) One alone shuts up well, but two shut up better
9) The undercover agent who falls asleep gets carried off to Tres Alamos
10) Better one airplane on the ground than a hundred flying
11) Breed soldiers & they'll kill your sons
12) When one cell is shut, two hundred open up
13) By your mouth you die
14) Don't look a gift Mercedes in the teeth

The original proverbs:
1) With guitar, it's another matter
2) In closed mouth no flies enter
3) In the house of the blacksmith, a wooden knife
4) See not, hear not, speak not
5) The monkey, though dressed in silk, is a monkey still
6) When the river resounds, it carries stones
7) One hand washes the other & both wash the face
8) One ox licks itself well, but two lick themselves better
9) The shrimp that falls asleep gets carried away by the current
10) Better one bird in the hand than a hundred flying
11) Breed crows & they'll peck out your eyes
12) When one door is shut, two hundred are opened up
13) By its mouth the fish dies
14) Don 't look a gift horse in the teeth

> *translated by*
> *Maria A. Proser, Arlene Scully & James Scully*

Notes:
mummy: rightist
Tres Alamos: a prison
Mercedes: Mercedes Benz, presently very fashionable among the upper
    echelons of the Armed Forces

Blood Knot

Between us, mother and son,
there is no line drawn.
You are my male face.

When you take my hand
my right hand takes my left.

Like a seismograph
you record my vibrations.

In your words you speak
what I remember.

Mastectomy

"Look at me."
Mother opened her robe.
I saw gardenias
blossoming
in place of breasts.

My skin pulls from stitches.
In the bedroom mirror
when I undress,
purple suture lines
carve
a sunken chest.

Le nageur noir traverse les profondeurs bleues
des jardins sous-marins du rêve mais les guerriers
qui protègent l'entrée du royaume de Guinée le renvoient
au pays des zombis où les chacals de la mort dévorent les
entrailles d'une femme famélique aux rythmes des tambours
de carnaval et des danses lubriques de Baron Samedi jetant
au feu le sel de la vie

a black swimmer crosses blue depths of underwater
gardens from a dream but warriors protecting the
entrance to the Kingdom of Guinea send him back to a
land of zombies where death jackals are devouring
the entrails of a half-starved woman to the drumbeat
of carnival and the lecherous dancing of Baron Samedi
throwing the salt of life on the fire

translated by Rosemary Manno

Le grand guignol du pays
ou
Le pays du grand guignol

le cirque et ses clowns
le théâtre et ses marionnettes
le carnaval et ses masques
le zoo et ses singes
l'arène et ses taureaux
l'abattoir et ses boeufs noirs
le yankee et la roue de l'argent
l'indigène et la roue du sang
le vodou et ses grands *Dons*
la sainte famille et ses démons
le peuple et ses malheurs
l'exil et ses sauveurs
sans foi ni loi
Haïti et sa croix
Haïti en enfer
au nom du père
du fils
et du zombi

The Grand Guignol of Countries
or
Country of The Grand Guignol

the circus and its clowns
the theatre and its marionettes
the carnival and its masks
the zoo and its monkeys
the arena and its bulls
the slaughterhouse and its black beef
the yankee and the money wheel
the native and the wheel of blood
voodoo and its grand Dons
the holy family and its demons
the people and their misery
exile and its saviors
without faith without law
Haiti and its cross
Haiti in hell
in the name of the father
and of the son
and of the zombi

translated by Rosemary Manno

The Meadow

this evening the meadow seems the essential thing
and because of it
what we talk about this evening
includes stalks and streams and frogs
and insects and eggs and blackbirds
and lack of worries about work contracts
rent contracts and other contracts
this evening
not far from us children are walking
hand in hand with their grown-ups
it is a meadow
true, there's a city on top of it

Cash Register

she wakes up
plagued by a body
that suddenly has eyes to see with
her head swims
plagued by impending sobriety
she puts on a white uniform
and tries to test her head's sorrow
till her senses resemble
ordinary receiving sets
and other mechanical furniture
in her technical apartment
she notes her name as usual
in her diary
not to forget her identity
not even when she squints her eyes
to see in her imagination the number of people
to whom she owes money and the amount of money
that people owe her
she momentarily sees all the oceans as a
peaceful part of the world that is blowing a
cloud
and recalls a garden's spiced
summer air
she uses a cup a spoon an egg-shell
as cold sterile instruments around her
breakfast
she does not sing
even if the stratum air around the factory masts
has run out of bird songs
and the radio has run out of batteries
and yet nothing has the tension of silence
she rubs her hands with lotion so they won't
rust

so they can smoothly continue
integrated with all the other machines
till they're worn through at the wrists
she packs her handbag
sets out on the road
that always leads straight to the shop with the cash register
where she sits working day after day
all these acts of preparation before the workday
begins
do not affect her
plaguing sobriety
which gradually increases as the hours
pass
and at five-thirty
she hurries home
with one of the shop's cheap bottles
of wine under her arm oh god

Ordinary Human Arms

we put our arms around each other
a pair of ordinary tax-paying human arms
not to rest them
but to harden them
a pair of ordinary concrete-accustomed
and marketed human arms
a pair of ordinarily needing
a pair of ordinarily hugging
human arms
we put them around each other
they are health-insured and ordinarily dressed
a pair of ordinary love-interpreting
human arms
how strong they are
sovereign, independent—
no matter where
no matter what the hour
no matter what the season
suddenly and for all time
human arms
without speculation
we put them around each other
as if to show that their powerlessness
doesn't exist

fillmo'e street woman

she is a dark woman
treading water
in a life of hard choices.
wrong decisions
limited alternatives
stockpens are embedded
in her eyes and mouth.

once she knew she was beautiful.

if you look closely
you can still feel
the edges of the fire that burned
in her eyes, on her skin
in the way her back arched
across fillmo'e street corners.

she wore her nails
sculpted in red
in those days
when that street
when this street
was ours

she sat on a barstool
snapped her fingers
and hunched her shoulders
as smoke rose between
the bandstand and counter
and the scene
got hot and sultry
and the music
pressed out the doors
and down the street.

further down
she slid in at jacks
had another cigarette lit,
flashed her teeth, laughed
as the club spun tight
shoulder to shoulder
thick smoke and blaring saxophone.

then she checked in with minnie,
bought a pitcher of beer and half-way
listened to some crazy poets
chant a continent of promises
with congo drum and shakere
punctuating the rhythms
and a flute solo
bursting out over
the tastiest of love poems

maybe, maybe
she slipped into connies
for some curried goat and coconut bread
or sweated spices next door
as leonard pulled another
sweet potato pie
out the oven and poured
his brown-red biting sauce
over smoking tender ribs
telling stories
as she savored another mouthful
then, when the street was ours.

she can see those days.
she knows them.
she remembers
before, before
imported cheese

before brandy filled truffles
before double lattes
hand-made paper cards.

she sits on the iron rimmed
privately owned bench
to rest her feet
and take the pinch
out of her back.
she holds the bitter in her mouth
sometimes spits it out at passers-by,
with steel in her stare,
there on that bench
on that corner
on that block
on that street
that was ours, that was hers
that was taken, that we let go
that is lost, that was fillmo'e
when the streets held the people
and the musicians had names
and the rhythm was blues,
and the downbeat was jazz
and the color
was black and fierce
like her.

the blood of Colorado miners
machinegunned down by Rockefeller's cops in 1914
forms abstract expressionist smears on canvasses hung
on the boardroom walls of Chase Manhattan Bank

you northamerican poets
masters of ennui-in-the-face-of-armageddon
welcome to the South African township of New Brighton
for the black workers of Port Elizabeth
a pile of rags by a dirt lot strewn with garbage
under a merciless streetlight near a row of scrapmetal huts
it's the body of a teenage boy shot through the chest
for singing walking in his brother's funeral procession
now tell the people here about your stalled aesthetics
your government grant your shattered linguistics
in the glare of Soweto and Sharpeville

there will be a time
when the world no longer maims us
no I mean they who after picking our pockets
knock us down and kick us in the head
that's why so many of us go along lame
you on one aluminum crutch and one stick picked up
from some waste place walking along in hunger and want
pain and deprivation warping your limbs
if all men were one man he would be you
dragging yourself along you pull us all forward

maybe because I stand behind
a cash register all day long my fingers black
from tearing the carbons from charge card forms
but the corner I look on seems every day more sapped
of spirit a concrete weight on my mouth
so I can't cry out and I wonder if it's money
that makes even those who have some
walk with a malnourished twist of gait
clutching their heavy burdens of shopping bags

Histories
Part I Europe and America

This is another landscape to be native to.
Dusk over the olive trees, the straight lines
of cypress, a scent of old sin beneath dim glass.
There are rabbits, and roses, and blue
fields of wheat: in your torn cotton stockings
you are trudging to the village
calling out the names of winds: sirocco, mistral.
Your card is the Carriage, sadness:
in the park, black carriages, driving in the rain.

But I could never second-guess the sky.
In my country the storms are nameless monsters, the landscape
immense. There are rattlers, and orchids, and history
goes off like an amateur's bomb.
Feeling all things to be possible
I am running barefoot across the desert
calling on the unpredictable light.
My card is the Train, danger:
on the edge of the horizon, the rails, beginning to burn.

Histories
Part II The New World

Cane grows there. The tired rocks. In the church
three flat faces carved into the walls say Egypt
was there. You harvest things. Under
the billowing sky you bend down
wiping your hands on your apron, pulling radishes
up from the black dirt. Repeating your story
repeating, it's
Judgment, what the old ones meant.

Water runs here. I sweat inside this cedar shack.
Elk hooves on my left hand stamp their memory into the dirt:
I'm not alone. Under the prairie sun
there is nowhere to hide
I push my hair back
gathering a song for the fight. It's
Deliverance: when the full moon comes.

It is so quiet where you are
it aches like temperance.
You were promised dust, and candles, and power
mediated through the cold hands of men.
You will outlive your firstborn, dying at last
from causes so natural they are not noticed.
You make the bread the centuries eat.
They see your lace and will remember
that one strand of red hair in the tarnished locket.

It's all so very clear here
it hurts like the primary colors
I was promised nothing
I demand it all
I will be split by lightning as the plain grows dark.

Cities will spring up here lit by greed and commerce
whose natives will be native to no place
whose women will walk all night over asphalt over
buffalo grass: seeing mirrors
they will remember God, her face
the horses running west till dawn.

El perro

Cercano al destacamento militar
un perro callejero fue muerto.
Era un perro flaco, pulgoso,
que los jefes militares creyeron
ser algún joven guerrillero
que pasaba orinándoles las carpas
convertido en perro desafiante.

Es la creencia, dicen las gentes,
que los soldados matan a los perros
porque aseguran que los guerrilleros
con su habilidad, saben convertirse
en palos, en piedras, en perros;
por eso casi nunca caen en combates
los guerrilleros en la montaña.

Pobres perros intranquilos
que sufren al igual que sus dueños,
una tortilla o dos al día
es su comida, y se les apalea
si invaden cocinas repletas
seducidos por el hambre.
Nunca comen carne, !ni en sueños!
como los gordos perros extranjeros.

Triste perro abatido a tiros,
no era un alto jefe guerrillero;
era simplemente un perro,
un perro callejero
de los muchos que transitan en el pueblo
y que sin malas intenciones
se paran, levantan la pata y orinan
los cuarteles de los asustados coroneles.

The Dog

Near the military barracks
a stray dog was shot;
it was a skinny cur, flea-ridden
which the military commanders
believed to be a defiant guerrilla
who changed into a dog
and urinated on their tents.

People say in the countryside
that the soldiers kill dogs
because they are sure the guerrillas
with their "nahuals" can turn themselves
into sticks, stones, or dogs;
and that is why so few guerrillas
are ever killed in combat.

Poor miserable dogs
who suffer the fate of their owners,
who a eat a tortilla or two a day
and who are beaten to a pulp
if they wander into the kitchen
overcome by hunger.
Not even in dreams do they ever eat meat,
like the fat foreign dogs do!

Wretched dog riddled with bullets,
he was not a top guerrilla commander,
he was just a dog, a stray mongrel
like many others who walk the dusty streets
and who without evil intent
stop to raise a leg and urinate
on the barracks posts of the frightened colonels.

translated by Victor Perera

Poem for Our Dog
Afraid of Thunder on a Rainy Day

I know what it is like to be so afraid
on a rain-soaked day such as this.
On a rain-soaked day such as this
in Viet Nam I prayed fervently.
In Viet Nam I prayed fervently
shivering uncontrollably in the mud.
Shivering uncontrollably in the mud
as men whose duty it was to kill me filed by
As men whose duty it was to kill me filed by
only a little more than a yard away
Only a little more than a yard away
on a rain-soaked day such as this.
The type of day that dogs don't understand.

Poem for U-Haul

The highway was made for a morning like this.
A woman with two sad blackeyes. Never
again, never, never again. Last night
was the last time, the last time, the last.

Sharks

When men purchase suits made from our skin
they become dukes, barons of giant corporations
with thousands of loyal employees producing
mirrors, locks, bibles, perfumes and
phosphorescent matches, all vital
for the survival of their countries.

Soup made from our fins makes men
want to slurp their way
up and down womens' calves.

Our jaws can provoke nightmares
a thousand miles inland, when displayed
dangling over the silver spoons, cameos
and other precious heirlooms
locked in glass cases, along
with the stale copies of Life
sleeping in the corners of antique shoppes
anywhere there is a Main Street.

Only gangs that are cool name themselves
after us, bold red letters
dripping blood down the backs
of their smooth black leather jackets.

We swim towards blood the way
some people cross an imaginary line
into the United States to pick lettuce,
or sink their hands into small oceans
of soapy water, bring dishes back to life
iridescent as oyster shells slurped dry
at a Republican fund-raiser for the governor
of California who will later pour gas

into the ocean and hand out match sticks.
Like the lettuce pickers and dishwashers,
all we are good for is fighting, trouble.
We carry fearsome switchblades, and
are born knowing how to use them.

Etymology: Chicano

Filemon says that when the movimiento began,
a talkshow host attempted to clarify
how the word "Chicano" originated.

A woman called in, assuredly said
it had its roots in "chicanery,"

those people being such liars and thieves,
so dishonest and deceitful.

What It Was Like

If you want to know what
it was like, I'll tell you
what my tío told me.
There was a truck driver,
Antonio, who could handle a
rig as easily in reverse as
anybody else straight ahead.

Too bad he's a Mexican was
what my tío said the
Anglos had to say
about that.

And thus the moral:

Where do you begin if
you begin with if
you're too good
it's too bad?

The Gloves

for Rhoda Waller

Yes we did march around somewhere and yes it was cold,
we shared our gloves because we had a pair between us
and a New York City cop also shared his big gloves with me
—strange, he was there to keep our order
and he could do that and I could take that
back then.

We were marching for the Santa Maria, Rhoda,
a Portuguese ship whose crew had mutinied.
They demanded asylum in Goulart's Brazil
and we marched in support of that demand
in winter, in New York City, back and forth
before the Portuguese consulate,
Rockefeller Center, 1961.
I gauge the date by my first child
—Gregory was born late in 1960—as I gauge
so many dates by the first, the second, the third, the fourth,
and I feel his body now, again, close to my breast,
held against cold to our strong steps of dignity.

That was my first public protest, Rhoda,
strange you should retrieve it now
in a letter out of this love of ours
alive these many years.
How many protests since that one, how many
marches and rallies
for greater causes, larger wars, deeper wounds
cleansed or untouched by our rage.

Today a cop would hardly unbuckle his gloves
and press them around my blue-red hands.

Today a baby held to breast
would be a child of my child, a generation removed.
The world is older and I in it
am older,
burning, slower, with the same passions.
The passions are older and so I am also younger
for knowing them more deeply and moving in them
pregnant with fear
but fighting.

The gloves are still there, in the cold,
passing from hand to hand.

Albuquerque, March 1985

Immigration Law

When I ask the experts
"how much time do I have?"
I don't want an answer
in years or arguments.

I must know
if there are hours enough
to mend this relationship,
see a book all the way to its birthing,
stand beside my father
on his journey.

I want to know how many seasons of chamisa
will be yellow then grey-green
and yellow
    /light/
        again,
how many red cactus flowers
will bloom beside my door.

I will not follow language
like a dog with its tail between its legs.

I need time equated with music,
hours rising in bread,
years deep from connections.

The present always holds a tremor of the past.

Give me a handful of future
to rub against my lips.

Albuquerque, October 1985

Then Comes A Day

The Resurrection Cemetery is an oasis of green,
encircled by the rising structures of the Edison
Utility Company and new roads interwoven through
the felled homes that once flowered with families.

The hills are sprinkled with the remains
of wood-frame shacks, splinters of the old
neighborhood that gentrification, progress,
and new "immigrants," this time with money,
have discolored.

It has been twenty years since I roamed these
earthen streets. Coming back, I am as new, alien,
except in that old cemetery where many of my
friends are buried: Dead by drugs, by gangs,
by police, by suicide, car crashes, and diseases
science conquered long ago.

In the end, what does it matter how they died!
The heart is only a beating thing. They left,
unconscious of the stars shimmering without them.
Still their time in the world echoes as secrets
in the rhythm of night. The earth may have their
fingers, but not what they touched: The contours
of skin beneath folds of an ocean's wave, the laminated
sweat on a brow—the sinew of an open-wound dream.

Every death was new life, becoming like the pacing
in a waking sleep that pounds into the realm
of impelling memory. So many funerals. So many dark
cruises through these curbless paths; revenge,
as thick as mud, in the windless air. All that's left
of that time are the headstones under sodden skies;

the bleeding of wombs as revolution is birthed
through an open-mouth scream. Coming back,
the quiet becomes relentless in the repose.

I have carried the obligation to these names.
I have honored their voices
still reverberating through me.
Even now, as the fight flourishes through
the burden of days, the rage has only
subsided to deeper seas.

Justice is the long, crevice-filled road
I've been stranded on all this time,
trying to reach a destination that climbs
uneasy over the horizon. I owe it to them
to stay. I owe it to them to await the daybreak
tearing out of the long night in the battlements.

And I can see the first light coming into view.
And I can hear their pleas through the hush.
And I remember: Twenty years come
that don't make a day,
then comes a day
that makes up
for twenty years.

The Concrete River

We sink into the dust,
Baba and me,
Beneath brush of prickly leaves;
Ivy strangling trees—singing
Our last rites of *locura*.
Homeboys. Worshipping God-fumes
Out of spray cans.

Our backs press up against
A corrugated steel fence
Along the dried banks
Of a concrete river.
Spray-painted outpourings
On walls offer a chaos
Of color for the eyes.

Home for now. Hidden in weeds.
Furnished with stained mattresses
And plastic milk crates.
Wood planks thrust into
    thick branches
    serve as roof.
The door is a torn cloth curtain
    (knock before entering).
Home for now, sandwiched
In between the maddening days.

We aim spray into paper bags.
Suckle them. Take deep breaths.
An echo of steel-sounds grates the sky.
Home for now. Along an urban-spawned
Stream of muck, we gargle in
The technicolor synthesized madness.

This river, this concrete river,
Becomes a steaming, bubbling
Snake of water, pouring over
Nightmares of wakefulness;
Pouring out a rush of birds;
A flow of clear liquid
On a cloudless day.
Not like the black oil stains we lie in,
Not like the factory air engulfing us;
Not this plastic death in a can.

Sun rays dance on the surface.
Gray fish fidget below the sheen.
And us looking like Huckleberry Finns/
Tom Sawyers, with stick fishing poles,
As dew drips off low branches
As if it were earth's breast milk.

Oh, we should be novas of our born days.
We should be scraping wet dirt
                    with callused toes.
We should be flowering petals
                    playing ball.

Soon water/fish/dew wane into
A pulsating whiteness.
I enter a tunnel of circles,
Swimming to a glare of lights.
Family and friends beckon me.
I want to be there,
In perpetual dreaming;
In the din of exquisite screams.
I want to know this mother-comfort
Surging through me.

I am a sliver of blazing ember
            entering a womb of brightness.
I am a hovering spectre shedding
            scarred flesh.
I am a clown sneaking out of a painted
            mouth in the sky.
I am your son, *amá,* seeking
            the security of shadows,
            fleeing weary eyes
            bursting brown behind
            a sewing machine.
I am your brother, the one you
            threw off rooftops, tore into
            with rage—the one you visited,
            a rag of a boy, lying
            in a hospital bed, ruptured.
I am friend of books, prey of cops,
            lover of the *barrio* women
            selling hamburgers and tacos
            at the P&G Burger Stand.

I welcome this heavy shroud.
I want to be buried in it—
To be sculptured marble
In craftier hands.

Soon an electrified hum sinks teeth
Into brain—then claws
Surround me, pull at me,
Back to the dust, to the concrete river.

Let me go!—to stay entangled
In this mesh of barbed serenity!
But over me is a face,
Mouth breathing back life.
I feel the gush of air,

The pebbles and debris beneath me.
"Give me the bag, man," I slur.
"No way! You died, man," Baba said.
"You stopped breathing and died."
"I have to go back!...you don't
    understand..."

I try to get up, to reach the sky.
Oh, for the lights—for this whore
        of a Sun,
To blind me. To entice me to burn.
Come back! Let me swing in delight
To the haunting knell,
To pierce colors of virgin skies.
Not here, along a concrete river,
But there—licked by tongues of flame!

The Blast Furnace

A foundry's stench, the rolling mill's clamor,
the jackhammer's concerto leaving traces
between worn ears. Oh sing me a bucket shop blues
under an accordion's spell
with blood notes cutting through the black air
for the working life, for the rotating shifts,
for the day's diminishment and rebirth.
The lead seeps into your skin like rainwater
along stucco walls; it blends into the fabric of cells,
the chemistry of bone, like a poisoned paintbrush
coloring skies of smoke, devouring like a worm
that never dies, a fire that's never quenched.
The blast furnace bellows out a merciless melody
as molten metal runs red down your back,
as assembly lines continue rumbling
into your brain, into forever,
while rolls of pipes crash onto brick floors.
The blast furnace spews a lava of insipid dreams,
a deathly swirl of screams; of late night wars
with a woman, a child's book of fear,
a hunger of touch, a hunger of poetry,
a daughter's hunger for laughter.
It is the sweat of running, of making love,
a penitence pouring into ladles of slag.
It is falling through the eyes of a whore,
a red-core bowel of rot,
a red-eyed train of refugees,
a red-scarred hand of unforgiveness,
a red-smeared face of spit.
It is blasting a bullet through your brain,
the last dying echo of one who enters
the volcano's mouth to melt.

Carrying My Tools

Any good craftsman carries his tools.
Years ago, they were always at the ready.
In the car. In a knapsack.
Claw hammers, crisscrossed heads,
32 ouncers. Wrenches in all sizes,
sometimes with oil caked on the teeth.
Screwdrivers, with multicolored
plastic handles
(what needed screwing got screwed).
I had specialty types: Allen wrenches,
torpedo levels, taps and dies.
A trusty tape measure.
Maybe a chalk line.
Millwrights also carried dial indicators,
micrometers—the precision kind.
They were cherished like a fine car,
a bottle of rare wine,
or a moment of truth.
I believed that anyone could survive
without friends, without the comfort of blankets
or even a main squeeze
(for a short while anyway).
But without tools...now there was hard times.
Without tools, what kind of person could I be?
The tools were my ticket to new places.
I often met other travelers, their tools in tow,
and I'd say: "Go ahead, take my stereo and TV.
Take my car. Take my toys of leisure.
Just leave the tools."
Nowadays, I don't haul these mechanical implements.
But I still make sure to carry the tools
of my trade: Words and ideas,

the kind no one can take away.
So there may not be any work today,
but when there is, I'll be ready.
I got my tools.

La tierra es un satélite de la luna

El Apolo 2 costó más que el Apolo 1
el Apolo 1 costó bastante.

El Apolo 3 costó más que el Apolo 2
el Apolo 2 costó más que el Apolo 1
el Apolo 1 costó bastante.

El Apolo 4 costó más que el Apolo 3
el Apolo 3 costó más que el Apolo 2
el Apolo 2 costó más que el Apolo 1
el Apolo 1 costó bastante.

El Apolo 8 costó un montón, pero no se sintió
porque los astronautas eran protestantes
y desde la luna leyeron la Biblia,
maravillando y alegrando a todos los cristianos
y a la venida el papa Paulo VI les dio la bendición.

El Apolo 9 costó más que todos juntos
junto con el Apolo 1 que costó bastante.

Los bisabuelos de la gente de Acahualinca tenían menos
        hambre que los abuelos.
Los bisabuelos se murieron de hambre.
Los abuelos de la gente de Acahualinca tenían menos
        hambre que los padres.
Los abuelos murieron de hambre.
Los padres de la gente de Acahualinca tenían menos
        hambre que los hijos de la gente de allí.
Los padres se murieron de hambre.

The Earth Is A Satellite Of The Moon

Apollo 2 cost more than Apollo 1
Apollo 1 cost plenty.

Apollo 3 cost more than Apollo 2
Apollo 2 cost more than Apollo 1
Apollo 1 cost plenty.

Apollo 4 cost more than Apollo 3
Apollo 3 cost more than Apollo 2
Apollo 2 cost more than Apollo 1
Apollo 1 cost plenty.

Apollo 8 cost a fortune, but no one minded
because the astronauts were Protestant
they read the Bible from the moon
astounding and delighting every Christian
and on their return Pope Paul VI gave them his blessing.

Apollo 9 cost more than all these put together
including Apollo 1 which cost plenty.

The great-grandparents of the people of Acahaulinca were less
        hungry than the grandparents.
The great-grandparents died of hunger.
The grandparents of the people of Acahaulinca were less
        hungry than the parents.
The grandparents died of hunger.
The parents of the people of Acahaulinca were less
        hungry than the children of the people there.
The parents died of hunger.

La gente de Acahualinca tiene menos hambre que los hijos
de la gente de allí.
Los hijos de la gente de Acahualinca no nacen por hambre,
y tienen hambre de nacer, para morirse de hambre.
Bienaventurados los pobres porque de ellos será la luna.

The people of Acahaulinca are less hungry than the children
    of the people there.
The children of the people of Acahaulinca, because of hunger,
    are not born
they hunger to be born, only to die of hunger.
Blessed are the poor for they shall inherit the moon.

translated by Sara Miles, Richard Schaaf & Nancy Weisberg

Medicine Woman
—for Dovie

medicine woman they call me
as if I should like it
like the kids in school
who called me little white dove
from some stupid song
about one more Indian woman
jumping to her death
how come you have an animal name?
they asked me, how come?
and I went home to ask my father
how come, Dad, how come
I have an animal name?

now white women come into my shop
and ask me to bless their houses
(what's wrong with them, I want to ask)
name their grandchildren
(do I know your daughters?)
blow some smoke around
say some words, do
whatever it is you do
we want someone spiritual—
you're Indian, right?

right. my tongue is held
by their gray hair
they are grandmothers
deserving of respect
and so I speak
as gently as I can
you'd let me, a stranger,
come into your home, I ask

let me touch
your new grandchild
let me name
the baby
anything
that comes into my head?
I am not believing this
but they are smiling
and tell me again
we want someone
spiritual
to do it

I write to my father
how come you never
told me who we are, where
we came from?

Women keep coming into my shop
putting stones in my hands
Can you feel that? they ask
Of course I can feel it
I'm not dead, but that
is not the right answer

My father writes back
the garden is doing good
the corn is up
there's lots of butterflies
all I know is
we come from the stars.

Looking for Indians

My head filled with tv images
of cowboys, warbonnets and renegades,
I ask my father
what kind of Indian are we, anyway.
I want to hear Cheyenne, Apache, Sioux,
words I know from television
but he says instead
Abenaki. I think he says Abernathy
like the man in the comic strip
and I know that's not Indian.

I follow behind him
in the garden
trying to step in his exact footprints,
stretching my stride to his.
His back is brown in the sun
and sweaty. My skin is brown
too, today, deep in midsummer,
but never as brown as his.

I follow behind him like this
from May to September
dropping seeds in the ground,
watering the tender shoots
tasting the first tomatoes,
plunging my arm, as he does,
deep into the mounded earth
beneath the purple-flowered plants
to feel for potatoes
big enough to eat.

I sit inside the bean teepee
and pick the smallest ones

to munch on. He tests
the corn for ripeness
with a fingernail, its dried silk
the color of my mother's hair.
We watch the winter squash grow hips.

This is what we do together
in summer, besides the fishing
that fills our plates unfailingly
when money is short.

One night
my father brings in a book.
See, he says, Abenaki,
and shows me the map
here and here and here
he says, all this
is Abenaki country.
I remember asking him
what did they do
these grandparents
and my disappointment
when he said no buffalo
roamed the thick new england forest
they hunted deer in winter
sometimes moose, but mostly
they were farmers
and fishermen.

I didn't want to talk about it.
Each night my father
came home from the factory
to plant and gather,
to cast the line out
over the dark evening pond,
with me, walking behind him,
looking for Indians.

Hanging Clothes in the Sun

His youngest daughter helps him
wring the clothes
while his wife answers phones
for doctors. The washing machine
is broken again.

In the factory
where he etches pathways
onto silicon chips
he wears a white coat and pants,
special shoes
to protect the chips from dust.

This is the best job he's had.
Better than last year
when he sprayed lawns with poisons,
then set up little signs
warning others not to walk there,
his clothes saturated,
his asthmatic lungs
choking on the clouds
marked hazardous to pets and humans.

All summer, he'd had to refuse
his daughters' hugs until
he removed his poisonous clothes
on the back stoop. Tee shirt,
jeans, baseball cap,
he put them in a plastic bag,
and showered while his skin burned.

Before that it was asbestos.
Wrapped in plastic,
he'd remove the sagging ceilings,

the flaking insulation on basement pipes,
vacuuming to remove the tiny particles
that would lodge in the lungs.
They floated in dreams, followed him
like a swarm of invisible bees.

This job was better than that,
in spite of the tanks of solvents
leaking noxious fumes,
the paychecks that didn't stretch.
Better than working at the defense plant
across the lake, where Air Force personnel
checked his I.D. badge each morning,
where everything and nothing was secret.

He squeezes water
out of shirts and towels.
He knows he drinks too much.
He dreams of moving to New Hampshire,
where his people walked
for 10,000 years,
and where, he believes,
the water is still clean,
but up north, the Lancaster paper mill
spills dioxin into the Connecticut River,
and downstream, five young girls have surgery
to remove cancerous wombs.
Anyway, there's no money.

Now the washing machine
is spewing soapy water
onto the basement floor.
His daughter frowns determinedly
at the towel in her hands.
At five years old, she knows how to help,
squeezing out the dirty water,
hanging clothes in the sun.

Department of Labor Haiku

In the winter snow
the kitchens fill up with steam
and men out of work

Why They Do It

Uncle Jack drinks because he's Indian.
Aunt Rita drinks
because she married a German.
Uncle Raymond drinks
because spats have gone out of style.
Uncle Bébé drinks
because Jeannie encourages him.
Aunt Jeannie drinks because Bébé does.
Russell drinks because he's in college.
Uncle Jack drinks
because he's a perfectionist.
Dave drinks because he's out of work.
Aunt Rita drinks
because she's a musician.
Bert drinks because he's married to Rita.
Renny drinks
because he likes a good time.
Gil drinks because he always has.
Raymond drinks
because Marie's too smart.
Jack drinks because Florence won't.
Lucille and Bob don't drink
because everyone else does.
Raymond drinks because of all the women
he'll never have.
Dick just drinks to empty the keg.

My Daddy's Tattoo

Goose-stepping over the Pacific
in your dirty old work shirt,
proud and sea-sturdy, you old navy hull;
fathering me through shark-infested veins,
flying on the forearm mast
the bloody dagger and skull.

Scuttling on my scarred, sea-sick belly,
God knows I tried to be navy...
Mutiny! Feed the coward to the sharks!
Burn his bald-headed books,
cut the tongue out of his poetry,
strike the son-of-a-bitch from the log!

Drowning down, my skull weighted down,
your dagger stuck in my skull,
my bloodied memories rise, and splash
and lick your boots,
and I spy you, huge and global
flying at half-mast.

The Prisoners

for Victor Jara

The guards
   take their orders
from Pinochet, Marcos, Thieu…

'If the prisoners don't talk,
      pour pails down their throats'

It's torture.
   The prisoners,
they swell up like toads
   but
They don't talk.

Victor, do you hear them
   in the National Stadium
thousands, still
         singing, clapping
their rough hands resounding over the Andes …
From Santiago, in the spring,
   a friend
witnesses this,
writes:

'In the prison, anyway, my friend …witnessed
an execution (more than one, but this as you'll
see was something special). What happened was,
one of the soldiers in the firing squad refused to
shoot the man. And what happened then, was,
he was put up against the wall alongside the
prisoner, and together they were shot. You begin
to wonder, what kind of human being is this?

That he would choose to die, and die obscurely,
rather than kill a man. It's strange that there
should ever have been gods, they seem so chintzy
in the light of something like this.'

we read this, Victor,
   while you sing 'Las Casitas Del Barrio Alto'
on the stereo,
So high spirited and true
   even the children go around
                    singing it by heart

Now Sing

NOW sing: the guards howling
beat him with obscenities.
    But he did.
His legend is
He was singing
        Venceremos
when they shot him.
Even for them, it was too much

they killed him,
they couldn't kill him enough.

Victor Jara
      sin guitarra,
who'd held out with bloody stumps
                  and sung

The Day Of The Night

The day of the night
they arrested Fernando:
I'm lounging on a bench,
among retired old men
and purple flowers
in the Plaza de Armas.

A one-legged man
rolls his sleeves up
and hums: over
an iron water bubbler
bubbling over
his hands and forearms.
Having dropped his crutch
he's washing away.
The worn-out
blue of his shirt
is gray as the overworked sky.
He could be a cloud
      blue
bird with spindly legs,
standing, one leg
more or less straight,
the other tucked up
under its belly:
tossing a splat of drops
off, onto the packed dirt
under a huge leafy palm
that droops and crests
—but motionless—
in carbon monoxide
it can live with,
the way an oasis
lives with desert.

He will stand
72 hours, without
a thing to eat,
a black
hood over his head.

If we had wings, roots, petals
we would not be men.

Toque de Queda

Already the greengrocer's on Merced
is shuttered up.
    Who cares
now, if he charged too much,
or that his thumb worked greasy miracles
                    with scales

What few people are left
          are newspapers the wind blows
over and over. What difference is it
   what lies they told,
what stories
buried

That one, with the bundle tucked under his arm,
he was a child once
     clutching its pillow,
     His head's
          wrencht
over his shoulder, where the fear is

And the fat man with a limp, it's terrible
to see him hurrying!
He was not built for this
     but an easy chair, a sweet illegal
pastry: of sugar, flour, butter.
But with a hunger
   now
no black market can satisfy,
he drags and is swinging the leg
     as though it were young, gawky and flighty
        O so wild
as never could get enough out of life

First and Last Poems

for Violeta Parra

there is nothing romantic
about death   about pain
tears falling like soft clouds
like copper clouds   the color of rusted blood
the texture of fire

the first enemy is fear
the second   power
the third   old age

all my life   all those books   all those feelings
words thoughts experiences
to say such simple words   to feel
such simple things

your mountains like my own   like home
rows of dust   of light brown soil
as if a gentle wind could level them
could blow them away

the sea   touching my nostrils
filling them   a country of smell
of sound   of wine   flowers   of salt air
of early morning   opening and
opening   through my mind
my heart   the extremities
of my hands   my feet

if I were a bird and could float
dipping and weaving tapestries of air
and light   if we could fly together
like silver crows   birds of dream

until everything stops   is silent and
gentle   like your songs   your voice

but the world allows us nothing
the world is nerves   is fiber
dust and sand   the world changes constantly
nothing remains the same

I see you singing into the air
as if your voice could fly   be free
were there creatures above you
listening   fishing your gifts
from the breeze   was there a place
that could hold you   as you opened yourself
to it   as you went where no one else
could follow   where no one else
could see

> *each time I have loved*
> *I have left part of myself behind*
> *until now I am mostly memory*
> *mostly dream   what I have left*
> *I give to you   my last love*
> *my last song*
>
> *the total of all*
> *I have ever felt or known*

we grow smaller as we grow
as things empty themselves of us
and we   of them

it is so deep   this thing between us
no name can contain it
even time trembles at its touch

Grandfather Buffalo

I saw them staring at him
in the mall   I was small
and holding his granite hand
his skin was bronzed
straight blue-black hair
his eyes and nose slightly curved
towards earth

I knew what was in their stares
an old Indian coin
a fat-lipped feathered caricature
a Cleveland team name
a wooden carving in an antique store
the relief of a bygone bus token
they saw the logo of Omaha
sponsor of nature shows
visions of Geronimo
parading in the circus
they were unbelieving
first-time gazes
colored by amazement

truth looked like a buffalo
a tall wide block that walks
like a stampede   desert soil skin
lungs that puff great mists
and appaloosa legs
that can outrun tornadoes

grandfather Buffalo
never stared back
never turned back the stares

of the wake we made
in our stampeding walk
through the mall

Postcard

just a quick note Ishi

I took my son to the Museum of Natural History
we looked for your long black hair
in the glass encasements of mothballed worlds
we listened for the clacking speech of your bones
among the fossils of grandfather-whales
who still sing their ancient songs
into the awestruck eyes of children

we did not find you amid the white
tanned painted mannequins dressed
like powwow tourists in sacred clothes

nor were you one of the Melanesians
Africans or Aboriginals standing stiffly
and dusty like taxidermic trophies

there were no Vikings or Druids
making human sacrifices   pillaging
the corners of a yet undying world
which leads me to wonder
who would exclude themselves   Ishi

we did not find you weaving
baskets or chipping arrowheads
stored among silk plants and crowds
too noisy to hear the wind
caressing the mountains of your Yana tomb
so we left saddened

because even here   among the trophy cases
the strand of web that wove your people
was cut from the fabric of this torn world
secretly   we were glad not to find you
frozen there   still weaving and carving
looking like Spider Woman cocooned
in her own web

Blue Cloud Rides Horses

blue cloud rides horses behind the wheel
of his chevy el camino with the hurst
four-on-the-floor

blue cloud rides psychedelic horses
and some made of remembered pain

blue cloud rides horses that leave hoof trails
up and down his atrophic veins

blue cloud rides cellblock horses
made of steel bars and thick walls
and when he gets out he rides horses again

blue cloud rides his baby's horse
and it makes him cry and it makes him cry
and it makes him want to forget
and makes him want and want and nearly die of want

blue cloud rides horses he thinks he hates
named officer   custer   john smith
de soto   jefferson   jackson   lincoln
columbus   cortez   and BIA

blue cloud rides horses he remembers he loved
named gin for the father he loved
named wild irish rose for the mother he loved

blue cloud rides ephemeral horses
sewn from dreamskin and old chants
named blue cloud and red cloud and white cloud
and grey clouds that rain faded dreams

blue cloud rides wind war-horses
on the ghost breezes
of the little big horn's plains
and he always wins   and he always wins

blue cloud rides horses that ride him
harder and faster to the vanishing haze

For cousin-brother Mandis

VII   The Pumpkin Field

An Army Lieutenant observes the Cherokees he guards
on their passage to the west, Arkansas 1838

What a grand lot they were,
　　　　the Cherokees I first saw in June,
lined up in their Georgian camp
　　　　to greet the chief on their departure,
elegant blankets hanging loose
　　　　about their shoulders, ramrod-straight,
dark eyes darting from high-boned
　　　　copper faces under bright turbans
and striped caps pulled down at an angle,
　　　　some in long robes, some in tunics,
all with sashes or wondrous drapery,
　　　　they stood, framed by bearded oaks,
Old Testament patriarchs
　　　　pausing on their way to the Promised Land.

Then in October, where I'd been sent ahead
　　　　to patrol their passage here in Arkansas,
they came from a cold and threadbare wood,
　　　　thin pines bent and tipped with sleet,
eyes glazed and blank,
　　　　half-naked, barefoot,
bones poking through
　　　　their scarecrow shredded clothing,
and stumbled through layers of mist
　　　　onto a scraggly open field
where in wet and tangled grass
　　　　fat pumpkins lay in rows
like painted severed heads.

Oblivious to all around them,
       skeletal automatons,
the Cherokees plunged ahead
       until a farmer on the edge
bade them halt
       and, breaking off a pumpkin,
invited them to take
       whatever his poor field could offer.

Flies swarming to their target,
       they darted up and down the rows,
black hair flying,
       long-nailed tentacles
protruding, they ripped apart
       the pumpkin flesh
until their brown and vacant
       faces merged with jagged pulp,
seeds foaming from
       their hungry mouths, and all I could see,
as on some battlefield, was
       everywhere a wasted mass of orange flesh.

A light rain then began to fall
       as if the shredded pumpkin fiber
drifted down around us:
       I felt ill
and sensed that cholera
       had set in. The farmer guided
me inside his cabin
       and put me down in a dark corner
where between the logs
       I could empty my stomach.

All night long I lay there
       while wind roared
and rain beat down
       and through it I could hear the sloshing

of the weary feet,
        the creak and rattle of ox-carts,
the cursing of the drivers,
        cracking their long whips to urge the oxen on,
the whinnying of horses
        as they struggled through the mud.

"What have we done to these people?"
        I cried out . . . And then a silence fell;
across the dark I saw
        row after row of pumpkins carved and slit,
their crooked eyes
        and pointed teeth all candle-lit within,
not pumpkins but death's-heads they were
        with features of the vacant
hungry faces I had seen,
        stretching to infinity
and glowing in the dark—
        and glowing still when I awoke—

as they do now, and as they always will.

XVI   The Burning of Malmaison

Greenwood, Mississippi
March 31, 1942

iii

In March twenty years later, in the brambles that had
overgrown the family cemetery, two Boy Scouts
came upon the headstone that read:

Greenwood LeFlore

Born June 3, 1800
Died August 31, 1865

The last chief of the Choc-
taw Nation east of the
Mississippi River

and seeing that the earth around it had been recently
disturbed, alerted the family, who days
later had diggers

go down to a depth of eight feet where they found
only three pieces of yellow pine,
broken but intact,

that had perhaps enclosed the grave,
but the coffin, and, with it, the remains,
the skull and bones

of the Choctaw chief, had disappeared.
Beside the headstone in the orange clay
the diggers unearthed a thin blue vein,

a remnant surely of the stars and stripes
    so dear to the Choctaw chief,
    who, when he was dying,

had asked his granddaughters to come
    and hold the flag above him,
    which they did, and they granted

him his dying wish, to have it wrapped
    around him in his grave, and of it now
    all that was left: this small blue stain.

Los pesares juntos

Aquí
hijas del verbo: madres, los esperaremos.

Escúchennos, "vivos se los llevaron y vivos los queremos",
recuérdenlo en el nombre del padre, del hijo y del hermano
detenidos y desaparecidos.

Esperaremos con la frente en alto
punto por punto unidas como la cicatriz a sus costuras.

Nadie podrá destruir ni desarmar nuestros pesares juntos.
Amén.

The Common Grief

We
daughters and mothers of the word
wait for them
here.

Hear us. "Alive they took them, alive we want them back."
Heed us, in the name of the father and the son and the brother
detained and disappeared.

We wait with heads unbowed
fused stitch by stitch like a scab to the sutures of a wound.

No one can sever or divide our common grief.

Amen.

Translated by Jo Anne Engelbert

Recuerdos número 1 - 2

A Roberto Armijo y Alfonso Quijada Urías

Mi primer recuerdo
parte de un farol a oscuras y se detiene
frente a un grifo público goteando al interior de una calleja
muerta.

Mi segundo recuerdo
lo desborda un muerto,
una procesión de muertos violentamente muertos.

Memories Numbers 1 - 2

To Roberto Armijo and Alfonso Quijada Urías

My earliest memory
starts at a burnt-out streetlight
and ends at a public spigot dripping
in a dead alley.

My second memory trickles from a corpse
a procession of corpses violently dead.

Translated by Jo Anne Engelbert

Envío

No pretendo sino que algún día
el dueño de la pobre pulpería
haga de mis escritos
los cucuruchos de papel
para envolver su azúcar y su café
a las gentes del futuro
que ahora por razones obvias
no saborean su azúcar ni su café.

Dispatch

I content myself that some day
the owner of this poor grocery store
will make paper funnels
out of my writings
to wrap up his sugar and his coffee
for people of the future
who now for obvious reasons
cannot savor his sugar or his coffee.

translated by Darwin J. Flakoll

Las tías

Siempre salían juntas cada tarde.
Iban a los cafés, los grandes almacenes—todo a su alrededor
era una pajarera—
Otras veces tomaban té en el patio
y hablaban, siempre hablaban con ligera inquietud:
el recuerdo de una elección difícil, aún dudosa.
Se hablaba. De ellas siempre, siempre de ellas, voraces, delicadas.
Sus miradas resbalaban sobre las apariencias,
las máscaras de las cosas (era un encanto o una ilusión?)
Se quedaban ahí sentadas, dotadas de un falso brillo,
una frescura sin vida, durante horas, tardes enteras hablando
de las cosas,
los sentimientos, el amor, la vida.
Ese era su dominio.
Y hablaban, siempre hablaban repitiendo, dándole vuelta a
lo mismo,
haciendo correr sin cesar entre sus dedos esa materia
extraída de su vida, amasándola, estirándola
hasta formar entre sus dedos un montoncito, una bolita gris.

The Aunts

They always went out together every afternoon.
They went to cafes, department stores—everything around them
was a bird cage—
At other times they had tea on the patio
and they talked, they always talked with a slight uneasiness:
the memory of a difficult choice, still doubtful.
They talked. Of themselves always, always themselves, voracious,
delicate.
Their eyes slid over appearances,
over the masks of things (enchantment or illusion?)
They'd remain sitting there, gifted with a false brilliance,
a lifeless freshness, for hours, entire afternoons talking about things,
about feelings, love, life.
That was their domain.
And they talked and talked, always repeating themselves, turning
the same things over,
ceaselessly running through their fingers the stuff
extracted from their lives, kneading it, stretching it
until they formed between their fingers a lump, a little gray ball.

translated by Darwin J. Flakoll

Pobres de nosostros

Nosotros moriremos con el Capitalismo,
estamos sentenciados.
Pobrecitos de nosotros
                    y sin haberlo disfrutado.

Poor Us

We'll die along with Capitalism,
we've been sentenced.
Poor us
          and without ever having enjoyed it.

translated by Darwin J. Flakoll

Asesinato del campeón de polo

Mataron al campeón de polo.
El hombre de mil trajes,
el mismo que tenía mansiones y yates
y novias ricas y bonitas en casi todo el mundo.

Lo mataron a balazos
y lo arrojaron maniatado
en una zanja.
Lo mataron porque dejó sus trajes,
sus caballos, el polo,
sus yates y mansiones,
y sobre todo porque después se puso a caminar
como pobre entre los pobres.

Assassination of the Polo Champ

They killed the polo champ.
The man of a thousand suits,
the one who had mansions and yachts
and rich, beautiful girl friends all over the world.

They shot him to death
and threw him hands tied
into a ditch.
They killed him because he left his suits,
his horses, polo,
his yachts and mansions,
and above all because he then started walking
as a poor man among the poor.

translated by Darwin .J. Flakoll

#3 de *Caballo de palo*

Lo conocí
viviendo
como una h encarcelada en la miel de sus abejas,
pero eran dulce amargo las rejas de la miel,
y por haberse enamorado
de la libertad
perdidamente,
y por no renunciar
a su amor ni ella a su amante,
la tierra para él
es huracán de estrellas perseguidas,
porque la libertad no puede ser
amante
sino de quien ama
a la tierra con su sol y su cielo.

#3 from *The Wooden Horse*

I came to know him,
living
like an h incarcerated in the honey of his bees,
but the bars of honey were bittersweet,
and because
he lost himself
in love with liberation,
and because he did not abandon
his love nor she her lover,
the earth for him
is a hurricane of persecuted stars,
since liberation cannot
love anyone
except whoever loves
the earth, with its sun and sky.

translated by Martín Espada & Camilo Pérez-Bustillo

#4 de *Caballo de palo*

Lo conocí
cojiendo
madrugadas de Lares despistado
por la majia morena de un requiebro de lunas
que corre
con un astro en los hombros,
remozado de ensueño,
como una mitolójica diosa de cucubanos.

Lo conocí
escuchando
indieras de tambores
montadas en recuerdos de caballos taínos
que atraen
las sicilianas en sus tardes de estiércol,
jugando alalimón con fuentes sin zapatos,
como alegres muchachas y muchachos
olorosos a frutas de noches deleitables.

Lo conocí
dejando
siestas de mariposas
para echarse
en la falda un racimo de cielo
que lleva
en el cuadril
un jirasol que canta
junto a la soledad carnal que se aúpa
en su estrella.

Lo conocí
velando
la bahía degollada por donde va

#4 from T*he Wooden Horse*

I came to know him
gathering
early mornings of Lares lost
in the brownskinned magic of quivering moons
that run
bearing a star on their shoulders,
rejuvenated in dreams,
like a mythic goddess of fireflies.

I came to know him
listening
to Indian ceremonies of drums
mounted on memories of Taíno horses
that lure
the Sicilian blossoms in their afternoons of manure,
playing a singsong game shoeless in the fountains,
like jubilant girls and boys
smelling of the fruit from delectable nights.

I came to know him
leaving
the siesta of butterflies
to toss
a handful of sky into the skirt
carrying
a sunflower that sings
in its folds
together with the solitude of the flesh hoisting itself
onto its star.

I came to know him
keeping vigil
over the beheaded bay

San Juan remando
sus amores, con Salomé en los ojos
de pueblos florecidos,
dando su testimonio de gracia anochecida
por el pavor de un beso acuchillado.

Lo conocí
ordeñando
cabras de retentiva histórica
como ondas rumiantes de mejillas taínas,
donde el atardecer de sus bocas rosadas
es una resonante jeneración de púrpura
que anda
ya por los astros con los pies en la tierra.

Lo conocí
soleando
el pensamiento en corrales de bruma
como una insurrección nueva de jirasoles,
tañedora de flautas de maíz
de entendimiento núbil,
que hace volar
la fe sobre marejada indócil de arcoíris.

Lo conocí
iniciando
piedras descamisadas en donde ya el estómago
no es
una frustración
hollando entre luciérnagas,
sino maizal que sube
la voz de sus espigas
hasta la resonancia
de un allá
empapado de pueblo.

where San Juan goes rowing
his lovers, with Salome in the eyes
of flowering peoples,
giving testimony of grace at nightfall
in the terror of a mutilated kiss.

I came to know him
milking
goats of historical memory
like musing waves of Taíno cheekbones
where the dusk of their pale red mouths
is a resonant blooming of purple
still walking
among the stars with feet on the earth.

I came to know him
sunning
intelligence in corrals of fog,
like a new insurrection of sunflowers,
playing corn flutes
of nubile understanding,
giving flight
to faith over a restless sea-swell of rainbows.

I came to know him
initiating
shirtless stones where the stomach
is not now
frustration
trampling fireflies,
but rather a cornfield that raises
the voice of its growing stalks
far off as the echo
of a distant place
drenched in the people.

Lo conocí
salvando soles osificados con la sangre purísima
que entona
la palabra
donde la muerte corriente
no excita
como el diamante que canta
para oír la canción de sus huesos.

Lo conocí
representando
imájenes de fragancias incrédulas
para fecundar
el óvulo del acto de entender
con células de eternidad brevísima
como el espacio cósmico
en expansión perpetua.

Lo conocí
dando
asilo a las menesterosas madrugadas que llevan
en los lomos la luz
doliente del descuido:
frío oscuro que jira
lentamente acabándose
como un cuerpo sensible
que ansía
la extinción de su muerte.

Lo conocí
defendiendo
a las piedras que velan
su mañana con la resignación
cabal de sus fulgores
—meditativos espíritus pétreos,
verdades de barro,

I came to know him
saving petrified suns with the purest blood
that intones
the word
where commonplace death
fails to excite
like the diamond that sings
to hear the song of its bones.

I came to know him
reflecting
images of incredulous fragrances
to fertilize
the ovum in the act of understanding
with cells of the most fleeting eternity
like cosmic space
in perpetual expansion.

I came to know him
giving
asylum to the destitute dawns that carry
the sorrowful light of neglect
in their loins:
cold darkness that whirls
slowly stopping
like a feeling body
that longs
for the extinction of its death.

I came to know him
defending
his morning with the consummate resignation
of his brilliance
to the vigilant stones
—rocky contemplative spirits,
truths of mud,

costillas lucientes
que hacen
despuntar la expresión que transforma
su ser a cada paso.

Lo conocí
sumerjiendo
su caballo de palo en el agua negrísima,
donde la fantasía relumbra
como virtud que cae
alzándose
hasta su frente injenua,
donde la muerte arquea
la sombra de su espejo.

Lo conocí
juntando
oes acometedoras con aes reproductivas
cuando el cielo
es la i numeral que destella
en el sexo cursivo de la e primorosa
como una u alterada con piernas de diamante
donde aprende
la lengua a dar
a luz por su espíritu orgánico.

Lo conocí
saliendo
de la cáscara oscura que cae
del sol
dormida,
como una propaganda etérea de ojos claros,
desapesadumbrada,
flotante,
como la piel feliz
del efluvio fragante

luminous ribs
that cause
the sprouting of the expression that transforms
its being at each step.

I came to know him
submerging
his wooden horse in the blackest water,
where the imagination gleams
like integrity that falls
raising itself up
to its ingenuous forehead,
where death bends
the shadow of its mirror.

I came to know him
fusing
active ohs with reproductive ahs
when the sky
is the number i that flashes
in the sexual script of the elegant e
like an altered u with diamond legs
where the tongue
learns to give birth
through its organic spirit.

I came to know him
emerging
out of the dark husk that falls
from the sleeping
sun,
like an ethereal proclamation of clear eyes,
without grief's weight,
floating,
like the jubilant skin
of sweet-smelling exhalation

de un presentimiento
que no se compadece
sino de su inclemencia.

Lo conocí
pereciendo
por el intacto vuelo:
latido soberano de elevación solícita,
piedra sensible con dureza de mar,
golpe que siente
el cristal eréctil de la forma,
corazón que golpea
su orijen en la sien.

Lo conocí
resistiendo
la obstinación amarilla del oro
—dúctil metal de terquedad de niebla—
que no deslumbra
a la atención que extiende
los brazos y estalla
como alba pertinaz
de azul acercamiento,
para que llegue
lo nuevo en lo acabado.

Lo conocí
tentando
la dureza paciente de ternuras calladas,
dolientes, como cielos doblados
que se echan
la tierra a la espalda
como inacabables seres que se yerguen
a enderezar los astros.

in foreboding
that does not pity itself
but rather its cruelty.

I came to know him
perishing
in his untouched flight:
lordly pulsation of anxious heights,
a feeling stone with the hardness of the sea,
blow that feels
the erect crystal of form,
heart that strikes
its origin in the brow.

I came to know him
resisting
the yellow obstinance of gold
—malleable metal with the stubbornness of fog—
that does not dazzle
the attentiveness that stretches
its arms and bursts
like a determined dawn
of approaching blue,
so that the new
begins in what has ended.

I came to know him
touching
the patient hardness of silenced delicacy,
sorrowful, like folded skies
that throw
the earth onto the back
like the endless beings that stand straight
to set the heavens upright.

translated by Martín Espada & Camilo Pérez-Bustillo

#35 de *La tierra prometida*

la tierra prometida
se
identifica
con las manos del peón desatendido
por el paladar
de la opulencia
con las manos
del peón
que
narran
la miseria social
que
rubrica
su cara profética
con las manos
del peón
que
compran
la alegría
empinando
el codo del amanecer
para dar
molde melódico
a la sensibilidad de su excelencia
con las manos
del peón
que
manejan
haciendas de cuchillos
para moldear
su aurora
con las manos
del peón

#35 from *The Promised Land*

the promised land
becomes
one
with the hands of the shunned peon
through the palate
of opulence
with the hands
of the peon
that
tell of
social misery
which
marks
his prophetic face in red
with the hands
of the peon
that
trade
in the joy
bending
the elbow of drunken daybreak
to give
melodic cast
to the sensibility of his excellence
with the hands
of the peon
that
manage
haciendas of knives
to mold
his aurora
with the hands
of the peon

que
truenan en los cartílagos del porvenir
con las manos
del peón
que
reprenden
a los orfebres de la depredación
para que no
se hurte
el sabor del saber
con las manos
del peón
que
dependen
del día de sus brazos
para
elevarse
en la mañana de sus piernas
sobre su sangre desbordada
con las manos
del peón
que
dependen
del día de sus brazos
para
elevarse
en la mañana de sus piernas
sobre su sangre desbordada
con las manos
del peón
que
son
rocío de poesía inusitada
con frescor de frenesí
perfecto

that
thunder in the cartilage of the future
with the hands
of the peon
that
push away
the goldsmiths of plunder
so that
the savored taste of knowledge
is not stolen
with the hands
of the peon
that
depend
on the day of his arms
to
rise
on the morning of his legs
over his brimming blood
with the hands
of the peon
that
depend
on the day of his arms
to
rise
on the morning of his legs
over his brimming blood
with the hands
of the peon
that
are
rainshowers of uncommon poetry
with a fresh breeze of frenzy
perfect

como violenta perturbación del ánima
que
abre
de par en par sus puertas
a los amaneceres
más insubordinados
con las manos
del peón
que
arrebatan
a lo porvenir
el porvenir
que
brama
persiguiendo
su brújula
con las manos
del peón
que
rechazan
henchir
sus pechos
de anchura anochecida
con las manos del peón
que
siembran
sentimientos de sol
para
ser
ruiseñor
que no
duerme
cantando
a su existencia
con las manos
del peón

like the violent confusion of spirit
that
opens
its doors wide
to the most
insubordinate sunrises
with the hands
of the peon
that
snatch
the future away
from what it would become
the future
that storms
following
its compass
with the hands
of the peon
that
reject
inhaling
dusky latitudes
with the hands of the peon
that
plant
sensations of sun
to
become
the nightingale
that does not
sleep
singing
to his existence
with the hands
of the peon

que
matriculan
el universo
para que
aprenda
a
cantar
como el peón del verbo subversivo
con las manos del peón
que
condecoran
su cuerpo maltratado
con tallos de estallidos
o truenos
desensillados
con las manos del peón
que
devoran
la bruma prejuiciada
de la posesión insensible
que
aúlla
como olfato de bestia malherida
con las manos del peón
que aun
se
reciben
de doctoras
en la universidad de la hoz
o del martillo
con las manos del peón
que
abogan
por
ciudadanizar
las ubres enamoradas

that
enlist
the universe
so that it would
learn
to
sing
like the peon of the subversive verb
with the hands
of the peon
that
dignify
his abused body
with sprouts of gunfire
or unsaddled
thunderclaps
with the hands
of the peon
that
swallow
the biased haze
of callous possession
that
howls
the sniffing of a badly wounded beast
with the hands of the peon
that still
receive
their doctorates
at the university of the sickle
or the hammer
with the hands of the peon
that
advocate
naturalization
for udders enamored

de la canción
de lo desconocido
con las manos del peón
que
agremian
jerundios de verbos ajitados
con las manos del peón
que no
enjaulan
agitaciones jóvenes
aun cuando
se les
ordene
o si no
serán
tiroteadas
o asesinadas
con las manos del peón
que domestican
neblinas bicéfalas
con las manos del peón pensador
que
son
las espaldas de la palabra
peón de la palabra
que la palabra
sea
tu peona

of the song
for the unknown
with the hands of the peon
that
unionize
gerunds of flurrying verbs
with the hands of the peon
that do not
cage
youthful agitation
even when
so
ordered
or else
to be
sprayed with bullets
murdered
with the hands of the peon
that tame
the two-headed clouds
with the hands of the thinking peon
that
are
the backbones of the word
peon of the word
let the word
become
your servant

translated by
Martín Espada & Camilo Pérez-Bustillo

Scene from the Movie GIANT

What I have from 1956 is one instant at the Holiday
Theater, where a small dimension of a film, as in
A dream, became the feature of the whole. It
Comes toward the end...the café scene, which
Reels off a slow spread of light, a stark desire

To see itself once more, though there is, at times,
No joy in old time movies. It begins with the
Jingling of bells and the plainer truth of it:
That the front door to a roadside café opens and
Shuts as the Benedicts (Rock Hudson and Elizabeth

Taylor), their daughter Luz, and daughter-in-law
Juana and grandson Jordy, pass through it not
Unobserved. Nothing sweeps up into an actual act
Of kindness into the eyes of Sarge, who owns this
Joint and has it out for dark-eyed Juana, weary

Of too much longing that comes with rejection.
Juana, from barely inside the door, and Sarge,
Stout and unpleased from behind his counter, clash
Eye-to-eye, as time stands like heat. Silence is
Everywhere, acquiring the name of hatred and Juana

Cannot bear the dread—the dark-jowl gaze of Sarge
Against her skin. Suddenly: bells go off again.
By the quiet effort of walking, three Mexican-
Types step in, whom Sarge refuses to serve...
Those gestures of his, those looks that could kill

A heart you carry in memory for years. A scene from
The past has caught me in the act of living: even
To myself I cannot say except with worried phrases

Upon a paper, how I withstood arrogance in a gruff
Voice coming with the deep-dyed colors of the screen;

How in the beginning I experienced almost nothing to
Say and now wonder if I can ever live enough to tell
The after-tale. I remember this and I remember myself
Locked into a back-row seat—I am a thin, flickering,
Helpless light, local-looking, unthought of at fourteen.

The Existence of Sarge

The old man places   his hat   on the table and
All three have sat down,   the same   as if their
Ancestors   had been   there first.   (Jump cut
To Sarge):   who is all at once by the booth in
Time   to hear the man   stricken   in years:
"Señor, buenos días."   On this   earth where
Animals   have crawled into men, Sarge is tall
Among them,   well past six-feet,   oppressive
Everywhere,   in a white shirt,   sleeves rolled
Up that declare   the beefiness   of his   arms
Which,   if extended, could reach across bodies
Of water.   He stands there   like God   of the
Plains country, heavy-footed   like a troglodyte,
And what he says   he says   with the weight of
A dozen churches   behind him: "You're in the
Wrong place, amigo.   Come on,   let's get out of
Here. Vamoose. *Ándale."*   The old man,   whose
Skin is second-stage bronze   from too much sun
That's gotten to it   and   won't pull back its
Color,   has   feebly   searched   among the
Threads of his pocket   and extracted   the sum
Of his need.   In quietude (etched in raw umber):
Reliquary   hands   are   endlessly   making   a
Wordless offering   in a coin purse.   Then the
Very way the tight-wound   voice   of Sarge
Echoes   through   the café walls, out onto the
Street,   and   back inside the Holiday Theater
Where I sit   alone   in the drop-shadows of the
Back—: "Your money is no good here.   Come on,
Let's go. You too,"   he says to the women,
Their torment half inside me.   And with that:
He plops   the old man's hat on his head   and

Picks him   up by the lapels.   *Put the film*
In reverse (I think).   *Tear out these frames*
From time-motion and color;   run   the   words
Backward in Sarge's   breath   and sever   the
Tendons   of his thick   arms   in bold relief.

Fight Scene Beginning

Bick Benedict, that is, Rock Hudson in the
Time-clock of the movie, stands up and moves,
Deliberate, toward encounter. He has come out
Of the anxious blur of the backdrop, like

Coming out of the unreal into the world of
What's true, down to earth and distinct; has
Stepped up to Sarge, the younger of the two,

And would sure appreciate it if he: "Were a
Little more polite to these people." Sarge,
Who has something to defend, balks; asks
(*In a long-shot*) if: "that there papoose down

There, his name Benedict too?," by which he
Means one-year old Jordy in the background
Booth hidden in the bosom of mother love of

Juana, who listens, trying not to listen. Rock
Hudson, his hair already the color of slate,
Who could not foresee this challenge, arms
Akimbo (*turning around*), contemplates the stable

And straight line of years gone by, says: "Yeah,
Come to think of it, it *is*." And so acknowledges,
In his heart, his grandson, half-Anglo, half-

Brown. Sarge repents from words, but no
Part of his real self succumbs: "All right—
Forget I asked you. Now you just go back
Over there and sit down and we ain't gonna

Have no trouble. But this bunch here is
Gonna eat somewhere's else." Never shall I
Forget, never how quickly his hand threw my

Breathing off—how quickly he plopped the
Hat heavily askew once more on the old
Man's head, seized two fists-ful of shirt and
Coat and lifted his slight body like nothing,

A no-thing, who could have been any of us,
Weightless nobodies bronzed by real-time far
Off somewhere, not here, but in another

Country, yet here, where Rock Hudson's face
Deepens; where in one motion, swift as a
Miracle, he catches Sarge off guard, grabs
His arm somehow, tumbles him back against

The counter and draws fire from Sarge to
Begin the fight up and down the wide screen
Of memory, ablaze in Warner-color light.

Fight Scene, Part II

Mad-eyed Sarge recovers with a vengeance, tears
Away his white apron, lays bare his words: "You're
Outta line, mister…" And there are no more words

To say when he crouches forward at the same time
That one punch crashes him rearward among the table
And chairs by the jukebox that breaks out into the

Drumming of "The Yellow Rose of Texas," who was,
It is said, dark-eyed herself. In the dynasty of
Towering men—: all height, all live weight has
Evolved into Sarge, who stays etched in my eye as when

He parts the air with a right cross…and Rock Hudson
Begins to fall, is falling, falls in the slackening
Way of a slow weep of a body collapsing, hitting

The floor like falling to the rocky earth, territory
To justice being what Sarge refuses to give up.
Rock Hudson, in the name of Bick Benedict, draws
Himself up, though clearly, the holding muscles of
His legs are giving out—one moment he is in a

Clinch with Sarge, the next he is rammed back
Against the red booths. The two of them have
Mobilized their arms that breed fire, and so it

Goes: a right upper-cut to Sarge and a jab to
Rock Hudson, engaged in a struggle fought in the
Air and time of long ago and was fought again this
Morning at dawn when light fell upon darkness and
Things were made right again. (I shut, now, slowly,

My eyes, and see myself seeing, as in a frame within
A frame, two fighters set upon each other. To this
Day I contend that I saw, for a second, the whole

Screen fill up with the arm-fist of Sarge blurring
Across it.) Now the fighters are one with the loud
Music bruising the eardrums. To be injured, there
Must be blood to see, for they have become two minds

Settling a border dispute. Two men have organized
Their violence to include me, as I am on the side
Of Rock Hudson, but carry nothing to the fight but

Expectations that, when it is over, I can repeat the
Name of goodness in Sarge's Place, as the singers sing
That raging song that seems to keep the fight alive.

Fight Scene: Final Frames

...And now it must end. Sarge with too much muscle,
Too much brawn against Bick Benedict with his half-idea
To stay alive in the fight, but his shoulders, all down
To his arms, can no longer contend to come back, cannot
Intercept the wallop that up-vaults him over the counter,

As over a line in a house divided at heart. He steadies
Himself upward, all sense of being there gone, to meet
Sarge *(upwards shooting-angle)*, standing with fists
Cocked to strike and he does, once more and again. You
Can see and can hear Rock Hudson's daughter give out a

Long-suffering cry, "Daaaddyyy!," and for Sarge to "leave
Him alooonnne!" But in a wrath like this there can be no
Pity upon the earth, as the blows come harder from Sarge
Like a fever in him. Then it happens: Sarge's one last,
Vital, round-arm punch, one just measure of power, turning

The concept of struggle around. The earth, finally, is
Cleared of goodness when Rock Hudson is driven to the
Rugged floor and does not rise, his wife, Elizabeth
Taylor (Leslie), kneeling to be with his half-life,
Illuminated body and heartbeat. Whose heartbeat? Whose

Strength must be summoned to make his graceful body
Arise? Who shall come forth and be followed? What
Name do I give thoughts that collapse through each
Other? When may I learn strongly to act, who am caught
In this light like a still photograph? Can two fighters

Bring out a third? To live, must I learn how to die?
Sarge stands alone now, with all the atoms of his power
Still wanting to beat the air, stands in glory like a

Law that stands for other laws. It remains with me:
That a victory is not over until you turn it into words;

That a victor of his kind must legitimize his fists
Always, so he rips from the wall a sign, like a writ
Revealed tossed down to the strained chest of Rock Hudson.
And what he said unto him, he said like a pulpit preacher
Who knows only the unfriendly parts of the Bible,

After all, Sarge is not a Christian name. The camera
Zooms in:

> WE RESERVE
> THE RIGHT
> TO REFUSE SERVICE
> TO ANYONE

In the dream-work of the scene, as it is in memory, or
In a pattern with a beginning and an end only to begin
Again, timing is everything. Dissolve and the music ends.

Era una escuadra desperdigada
(septiembre de 78)

Nadie quería cruzar aquel campo quemado.
(Las cenizas plateadas y algún destello rojo
de las últimas brasas).
Te tiraste de primero y tu cuerpo se miraba oscuro
contra lo blanco.
Escondidos en el monte los demás esperábamos verte
alcanzar la orilla
para irnos cruzando.

Como en cámara lenta lo recuerdo:
el terreno inclinado, resbaloso, caliente
la mano agarrada al fusil
el olor a quemado.
El ruido de las hélices
de vez en cuando, ráfagas.

Tus botas se enterraban en lo blando
y levantabas un vaho blanquecino
a cada paso.
(Debe haber sido un tiempo
que se nos hizo largo)

Todos los compañeros, Dionisio, te mirábamos
nuestros pechos latiendo inútilmente
bajo la luna llena.

It Was a Ragged Squadron
(September, 1978)

No one wanted to cross that burnt field.
(Those silver ashes with a red spark or two
        from the final embers.)
You went out first and your body looked dark
        against the white.
Hidden in the brush, we others waited
        until you made it to the other side,
then followed you.

I remember it in slow motion:
the sloping terrain, slippery and hot,
your hand around your weapon,
        the stench of fire.
The sound the propellers made,
sporadic bursts of gunfire.

Your boots sank into the pliant earth
and you raised a whitish mist at every step.
(Time must have slowed down for us.)

Dionisio, all the comrades watched you,
our hearts beating uselessly
        beneath the full moon.

translated by Margaret Randall & Elinor Randall

Querida tía Chofi

—a Adilia Moncada

No eras la tía Chofi del poema de Jaime Sabines,
pero también te llamabas Sofía, Chofi.
Vos, la rebelde desde chiquita,
la que se casó contra todo el mundo
pero con su hombre. Aunque la vida
. después resultara un purgatorio e infierno
hasta que Guillermo terminó desnucándose borracho
para tu descanso. Y concluiste
otro capítulo de tu vida
que yo te escuchaba contar, fascinada
mientras hacías escarchas de azúcar de colores
que secabas al sol en láminas de vidrio.

Artesana, Imaginera, Panadera, Decoradora,
poblaste tu mundo de enanos, Blancanieves,
Cenicientas, Niñas de 15 años,
Parejas de Primera Comunión, Casamientos
Tiernos de Bautizo,
entre tules, perlas, filigranas,
ramilletes, cintas y lazos de pastillaje.

Los sacuanjoches sacados de panas de agua
se convertían en tus manos en coronas,
diademas y cetros frescos
—efímeros símbolos de efímeros reinados.
Los mediodías eran la penumbra de tu cuarto
contra el solazo. Tu aposento lleno de pinceles,
óleos, moldes de yeso,
caballetes, lienzos, bastidores,
santos de bulto a medio retocar,
y en medio del caos, tu cama eternamente desarreglada.

Dear Aunt Chofi

You weren't the aunt Chofi of Jaime Sabines'[1] poem,
but your name was also Sofía, Chofi.
A rebel from birth
you insisted on marrying against all entreaties
but your man's. Even though life later became
a purgatory, a living hell
until Guillermo ended up breaking his neck
while drunk, to your relief.
So ended another chapter in your life
and I listened to you tell it,
fascinated as you dried your colored sugar frosting
on panes of glass in the sun.

Artisan, maker of religious images, baker, decorator,
you peopled your world with dwarfs, Snow Whites,
Cinderellas, adolescent coming out parties,
first communion duos, weddings,
tender baptismal figures,
among the tulle, the pearls and filigree,
bouquets, glittering ribbons and bows.

Cacalosuchil blossoms lifted from pans of water
became crowns in your hands,
diadems and magic wands
—ephemeral symbols of ephemeral kingdoms.
Noontime was the cool shade of your room
against a scorching sun.
Your habitat filled with brushes,
oil paints, plaster molds, easels,
canvases, canvas stretchers, statues of saints
in the process of coming alive,
and in the midst of all the chaos,
your eternally unmade bed.

[1] Mexican poet.

Habladora, Conversadora, platicabas mientras ibas
fumando cigarrillos,
encendiendo uno con la colilla del otro
hasta dejar tu cuarto como un cenicero lleno
de colillas retorcidas y fragante a tazas de café,
miel, azúcar, harina, claras de huevo,
trementina, aceite de linaza,
sábanas viejas.

Amazona admirable en tus fantásticas hazañas:
(amarraste al ebrio de tu marido,
te amaste con el primer Gurú legítimo de la India
que pasó por Managua).
Curandera, hacías medicinas, jarabes y pócimas terribles
que nos obligabas a beber
contra todas las enfermedades posibles.

Recorrías Managua bajo aquel solazo
con tu cartera repleta de chunches,
el pelo alborotado
y la eterna brasa entre los labios.

Qué necesidad, qué desgracia no ayudaste:
Partera, Enfermera,
alistabas muertos, atendías borrachos,
defendías causas perdidas desde siempre
y en todas las discusiones familiares
gobernaba tu figura desgarbada.

Siempre en tránsito, viviste
en cuartos alquilados,
te salvaste de milagro en los terremotos
y cualquier persona soportó cualquier barbaridad tuya.
Te peleaste hasta con la guardia
y fuiste a parar al exilio de México.

Always talking, conversing,
you'd go on about this and that
as you smoked your cigarettes,
lighting one with the butt of the last
until your room was an ashtray
overflowing with twisted stubs and fragrant cups of coffee,
honey, sugar, flour, egg whites, turpentine,
linseed oil, old sheets.

Admirable Amazon in your fantastic feats:
(you tied your drunken husband up and fell in love
with the first legitimate guru from India
to pass through Managua).
Witch doctor, you mixed medicines,
syrups and terrible potions you made us drink
against all possible diseases.

What need, what misfortune didn't you succor:
midwife, nurse,
you laid out corpses, attended drunks,
defended all lost causes
and in every family argument
your gawky figure ruled.

Always in transit, you lived
in rented rooms,
miraculously saved yourself in earthquakes
and everyone put up with your excesses.
You even fought with the Guard
and ended up exiled in Mexico.

A veces, con tus manos pequeñitas y regordetas
de puntas afiladas, como manos de bebé
o como palmeritas de abanico en miniatura,
te arreglabas el pelo entrecano
con una onda sobre la trente
y en ese gesto rápido, fugazmente
se vislumbraba tu antigua gracia.

Porque un día de verdad que fuiste hermosa,
morena y altiva.
Nada tenía que ver esa joven con vos misma:
Oveja Negra, Paja en ojos ajenos,
Vergüenza de tu única hija
—que a pulso enviaste a estudiar a México—
y de allí saltó a Pittsburgh, a New York,
y recorrió Europa acumulando becas
y títulos académicos
con nostalgias de supuestos linajes
para borrarte, para no vene,
para no tener que sufrirte.
¡Ah! pero vos te llenabas la boca con su nombre.

La mañana antes de tu muerte
estuviste igual que siempre, gritona y bocatera
sólo que te quejaste
de mucho malestar en los riñones.
(Tu hija supo la noticia en Buenos Aires).

Vos que me contabas de tus trances en el espejo,
tus reencarnaciones
—múltiples vidas de las que recordabas
incontables anécdotas:
(En una de tus vidas fuiste una niña que murió
recién nacida, en otra, un hombre aventurero…)

Sometimes you'd pat your graying hair in place
with chubby little fingers, like the tips
of baby's fingers or miniature *palmerita* fans,
touch that wave over your forehead
and in that brief gesture, fleetingly,
one glimpsed your younger grace.

Because truly, once you were beautiful,
dark haired and proud.
That young woman had nothing to do with who you were:
black sheep, a thorn in the eyes of others,
shame of your only daughter
—you slaved so she could study in Mexico—
who went on to Pittsburgh, New York,
traveled through Europe
accumulating scholarships and academic titles
with the nostalgia of a supposed lineage
so she could erase you, wouldn't have to see you,
wouldn't have to suffer you...
Oh, but how her name sounded on your lips!
The morning before your death
you were the same as ever,
vociferous and loud-mouthed,
only complaining of great pain
in your kidneys.
(The news reached your daughter in Buenos Aires.)

You, who told me about your perils in the mirror,
your reincarnations—many lives
from which you remembered
innumerable anecdotes:
(In one you were a little girl who died
at birth, in another an adventurous male...)

¿En qué vida estás ahora
que ya no te llamas Sofía,
          Sabia, Sabiduría,
ahora que te llamas huesos, madera desvencijada,
podredumbre, tierra vegetal,
humus, fosa, oscuridad,
                    nada?

Ahora que ya no estás, que ya no existís
quizás te reconozcas
                    en este espejo.

What life is yours today
in which you are Sofía no longer,
   Wise Woman, Wisdom,
now that you answer only to bones,
disjointed wood, decay, vegetal earth,
humus, grave, darkness,
     nothing?

Now that you no longer exist, exist no longer,
perhaps you recognize yourself
     in this mirror.

   translated by
   Margaret Randall & Elinor Randall

Precisamente

Precisamente porque no poseo
las hermosas palabras necesarias
procuro de mis actos
                para hablarte.

Precisely

Precisely because I do not have
the beautiful words I need
I call upon my acts
                  to speak to you.

translated by
Margaret Randall & Elinor Randall

Biographical Notes

Claribel Alegría was born in Estelí, Nicaragua in 1924, and grew up in El Salvador. She has long been recognized as a major voice in the struggle for liberation in El Salvador and in Central America. She has published over forty books including poetry, novels and a book of children's stories. Many of her books have been translated into English, including the Curbstone editions *Ashes of Izalco, Luisa in Realityland, Family Album, Fugues, Thresholds* and *Sorrow* (recipient of an Independent Publisher Book Award). Alegría has received several awards in Latin America and Europe, and her book of poetry, *Sobrevivo*, received a Casa de las Américas Prize. She is presented in the Bill Moyers "Language of Life" series that first aired on PBS in 1995. Claribel Alegría and her husband, Darwin J. Flakoll, collaborated on a number of testimonies: *Death of Somoza, Tunnel to Canto Grande, The Sandinista Revolution* and *They'll Never Take Me Alive*. Vividly documenting key dramatic events in Latin American history, these works have earned international recognition. Alegría and Flakoll also collaborated on their novel *Ashes of Izalco*, set in El Salvador in 1932, the year of the matanza. Claribel Alegría has continued to reside in Managua since Darwin Flakoll's death in 1995.

Doug Anderson holds an M.A. in playwriting from the University of Arizona, and has taught creative writing at a number of universities, most recently Pitzer College and the William Joiner Center summer workshops at The University of Massachusetts-Boston. In addition to three books of poetry, he has published fiction and criticism. His critical writings have appeared in *The New York Times, The London Times Literary Supplement*, and *The Boston Globe*. He won the Kate Tufts Discovery Prize for his book *The Moon Reflected Fire*, which was based on his experiences in the Vietnam War. His most recent book, *Blues for Unemployed Secret Police* was published by Curbstone Press with support from the Eric Mathieu King Fund.

Naomi Ayala's book of poetry, *Wild Animals on the Moon* (Curbstone Press, 1997) was selected by the New York City Public Library for the Best Book for the Teen Age list. Ms. Ayala began teaching at a Connecticut prison in her late teens and in the years that followed, while teaching in public schools, organized literary events throughout the state's correctional system. In addition to her work for the National Council of La Raza as curriculum developer and editor of English/Spanish texts, Ayala has received acclaim for her award-winning work in arts administration.

Jimmy Santiago Baca was born in Santa Fe, New Mexico in 1952. His books of poetry include *What's Happening* (Curbstone, 1982), *Martin and Meditations on the South Valley*, and *Immigrants In Our Own Land*. Baca's other works include *Working in the Dark: Reflections of a Poet of the Barrio* and the screenplay *Bound By Honor*, for the film of the same name from Hollywood Pictures. At present, he lives in Albuquerque, New Mexico.

Gioconda Belli was born in Managua, Nicaragua. Her poetry collection, *Línea del fuego* (Line of Fire) received the Casa de las Américas Prize, and in 1989 Curbstone published a bilingual edition of her poetry, *From Eve's Rib*. Her novel *La mujer habitada (The Inhabited Woman)* won the Prize for the Best Literary Work of the Year from the Union of German Publishers and Editors. At present, Belli lives in California with her husband and children.

Kevin Bowen is the director of the William Joiner Center for the Study of War and Social Consequences at the University of Massachusetts-Boston. His poetry collections include *Playing Basketball With The Viet Cong* and *Forms of Prayer at the Hotel Edison*. He has co-edited the anthologies *Writing Between the Lines: an Anthology on War and its Social Consequences* and *Mountain River: Vietnamese Poetry from the Wars, 1948-1993*. Most recently, with Nguyen Ba Chung, he co-translated the collection *Distant Road: Selected Poems* of Nguyen Duy. He lives in Dorchester, Massachusetts with his wife and two children.

Author of six books of poetry, **Ferruccio Brugnaro** was born in Mestre, Italy in 1936. He worked for more than 30 years—most of his adult life—in the giant complex of chemical factories in the Porto Marghera district of Venice. In 1975 his first volume, *Vogliono cacciarci sotto* was published by Bertoni, and in 1977 a selection of his poetry was set to music by the songwriter Gualtiero Bertelli. With other workers, he began publishing the workers' writings, "abiti lavoro" in the 80s. *Fist of Sun* (Curbstone, 1998) contains selections from three of Brugnaro's major works—*We Should Affirm, The Silence Doesn't Rule,* and *The Clear Stars of These Nights*. He retired from factory work in 1992 and now devotes full time to his writing.

Julia de Burgos (1914-1953) completed her higher education at the University of Puerto Rico in 1933. After teaching in rural schools, she worked as a writer for a radio program but was fired for her political activism on behalf of independence for Puerto Rico. In her lifetime, she saw only two of her books in publication, *Poem in Twenty Furrows* (1938) and *Song of the Simple Truth* (1939), but the poet is posthumously revered in Puerto Rico. In 1996, Curbstone Press published *Song of the Simple Truth: The Complete Poems* of Julia de Burgos in a bilingual edition translated and with an introduction by Jack Agüeros.

Ernesto Cardenal was born in 1925, in Granada, Nicaragua. In 1965 he was ordained a priest. An early advocate of liberation theology, he fought for political freedom through his religious work and was declared an outlaw by the dictator Anastasio Somoza in 1977. After the Sandinista triumph, he served as Minister of Culture from 1979 to 1988. He is currently director of La Casa de los Tres Mundos, a cultural organization in Granada, Nicaragua. Cardenal is the author of numerous volumes of poetry including: *Zero Hour, Flights of Victory, Homage to the American Indians, Golden UFOs*, and *Cosmic Canticle*.

John Carey's book of poems, *Hand to Hand*, was published by Curbstone Press in 1983. Born in 1958, Carey at present practices medicine in Willimantic, Connecticut. He is also a musician, playing country and blues guitar.

Otto René Castillo (1936-1967) was a guerrilla and poet in Guatemala. His political activities began in 1954 as a young student organizer, and he began to write poetry that same year after he was exiled from Guatemala for the first time. During the next ten years he was frequently imprisoned, tortured, and exiled. On his final return to Guatemala in 1966, he joined the Armed Revolutionary Front. In March of 1967, he and his guerrilla group were ambushed and captured. He was put to death on March 19, 1967. *Let's Go!*, a selection of his poetry, was published by Curbstone Press in 1984.

Currently Poet Laureate of Connecticut, **Leo Connellan** has published twelve books of poetry, including *Maine Poems, Short Poems, City Poems, Provincetown*, and *The Clear Blue Lobster-Water Country*. Winner of numerous prizes, including the Shelley Memorial Award, he is also poet-in-residence for the Connecticut State University system. Originally from Maine, Connellan now resides in Hanover, Connecticut, with his wife Nancy.

Roque Dalton (1935-1975) of El Salvador was enormously influential in the history of Latin America as a poet, essayist, intellectual, and revolutionary. In his brief life, he wrote eighteen volumes of extraordinary poetry and prose, one of which (*Taverna y otros poemas*) received a Casa de las Américas poetry prize in 1967. His autobiographical novel, *Poor Little Poet That I Am*, is forthcoming from Curbstone Press. His legacy extends beyond his achievements as a poet to his political writings and his work in the establishment of the ERP (People's Revolutionary Army) in El Salvador. He was murdered by a faction of the ERP in 1975.

Nguyen Duy's given name is Nguyen Duy Nhue. He was born on December 12, 1948, in Dong Ve village, Thanh Hoa province. He now lives in Ho Chi Minh City. He holds a degree in Vietnamese linguistics and literature. In 1965 he served as a militia squad leader, defending the area of Ham Rong-Thanh Hoa. Since 1977, he has been the representative of the newspaper *Van Nghe* in South Viet Nam. Among his published works are ten collections of poetry, three collections of memoirs, and a novel, and Curbstone published a bilingual selection of his poetry, *Distant Road,* in 1999. Among his awards are the poetry prize of *Van Nghe* in 1973 and the poetry prize of the Vietnam Writers' Association in 1985.

Don Gordon (1902-1989) was born in Bridgeport, Connecticut. Author of five poetry collections, Gordon was blacklisted during the McCarthy era. His last book, *The Sea of Tranquillity*, was published by Curbstone Press just weeks before his death, at the age of 87.

Maketa Groves was born and raised in Detroit, Michigan. Her poems have appeared in a number of magazines and anthologies. Her debut book of poetry, *Red Hot on a Silver Note* (Curbstone Press, 1997), won the PEN/Oakland Award for Excellence in Literature. Currently, Maketa Groves lives in Los Angeles where she teaches and continues to write.

Joan Joffe Hall taught creative writing and women's studies at the University of Connecticut until her recent retirement. Her books of poetry include *The Rift Zone* and *Romance and Capitalism at the Movies*. In 1991, Kutenai Press published *Summer Heat*, a collection of her short stories.

Juan Felipe Herrera received a Before Columbus Foundation American Book Award for *Facegames*. He has since published several books of poetry including *Night Train to Tuxtla* from the University of Arizona Press, and *Love After the Riots* from Curbstone Press. He teaches at California State University at Fresno.

Born in New York City in 1933, **Jack Hirschman** has lived since 1973 in San Francisco. He is editor of *Art on the Line*, a collection of essays by artists describing how and where their art intersects with politics, and an anthology of Haitian poetry, both of which are forthcoming from Curbstone Press. He currently assists in the editing of the journal *Left Curve*, and has been active in the Coalition of Writers Organizations (COWO). Among his many volumes of poetry are *A Correspondence of Americans, Black Alephs, Lyripol, The Bottom Line*, and *Endless Threshold*. His works have recently been translated into Italian and French.

Efraín Huerta (1914-1982) was born in Silao, Guanajuato, Mexico, in 1914. He worked for several years as a journalist in Mexico City, specializing in film criticism. A member of the literary group centered around the journal *Taller* in the late 1930s, he remained faithful until the end of his life to this initial orientation, always seeking a poetic expression fusing eroticism with political rebellion. During a career that culminated in the receipt of the Villaurrutia Poetry Prize in 1975, the National Literature Prize in 1976, and the National Journalism Prize in 1978, Huerta was the major Mexican poet most openly committed to far-reaching sociopolitical change. He died in Mexico City in 1982. A complete collection of Huerta's poems, *Poesía completa*, was published in Mexico in 1988.

Teresa de Jesús is the pseudonym of a Chilean poet who lives in Santiago. Her poems, which were smuggled out of the country, testify to the aftermath of the 1973 military coup, and were published by Curbstone in her first book, *De Repente/All of a Sudden* (1977). In 1988, the University of Oslo published her book, *El reino del candado/The Kingdom of the Lock*, which contains poems about the disappearances of political prisoners during the Pinochet dictatorship. In 1993, her book of poetry, *Túneles y jualas/Tunnels and Cages*, appeared in Chile.

Born in 1938, **Eileen Kostiner** began writing in her thirty-eighth year when the Women's Movement encouraged her to speak in her own voice. Curbstone Press published her first book, *Love's Other Face*, in 1982.

Paul Laraque was born in Jérémie, Haiti, on September 21, 1920. Under the pen name of Jacques Lenoir, he published many poems in the Haitian literary magazine *Optique* (Port-au-Prince, 1954-57). In 1964, he was deprived of his Haitian citizenship by the Duvalier dictatorship. He was the first author writing in French to win the Casa de las Américas prize (1979). At the end of the Duvalier dynasty in 1986, Paul returned to Haiti after 25 years in exile. Former secretary-general of the Association of Haitian Writers Abroad, he is the author of several poetry books in French and Creole, some of which have been translated into Spanish, English, and Italian, including *Camourade* (Curbstone, 1988). He was again exiled with the overthrow of Jean-Bertrand Aristide as president of Haiti in 1991, and the murder of the poet and essayist Guy F. Laraque, Paul's brother. His latest book is *Oeuvres Incomplètes* (1999). He is currently working in collaboration with Jack Hirschman on a bilingual anthology of Haitian Creole poetry, *Open Gate* (Curbstone, 2001), and *Liberty Drum*, a new selection of his French and Creole poems.

Born in 1951 in Kalundborg, Denmark, **Marianne Larsen** made her literary debut in 1971 with the poetry collection *Koncentrationer* (Concentrations). Since then she has published several collections of poetry. Her major works include *Billedtekster* (Visual Text), *Modsætninger* (Contrasts), *Handlinger* (Acts), *Der er et håb i mit hoved* (There is a Hope in My Head). Her latest works of poetry are *Paratkërlighed* (Ready-Made Love, 2000) and *Lille Dansk Sindssjournal* (Little Danish Mental Journal, 1998). Currently, she lives in Copenhagen and devotes full time to her writing.

devorah major is a poetry, fiction and essay writer from San Francisco, where she works as an editor and arts administrator. In 1989 her first book of poetry, *traveling women*, a two-poet anthology with Opal Palmer Adisa, was published by Juke Box Press. Her second book of poetry, *street smarts*, was published by Curbstone Press in 1996. Her first novel, *An Open Weave*, also published in 1996, was awarded the First Novelist Award from the American Library Association's Black Caucus. She is currently at work on a second novel.

Rigoberta Menchú, recipient of the Nobel Peace Prize in 1992, began her social and political activity at an early age in Guatemala. Her writings express a search for justice as well as a deep religious belief. At present she continues her work through the Vicente Menchú Foundation, a human rights organization that supports the rights of indigenous peoples of Guatemala and other countries.

Born in Chicago in 1946 and raised in Reno, Nevada, **Sarah Menefee** has published widely. Her collections of poetry include *I'm Not Thousandfurs* and *The Blood About the Heart* (both from Curbstone Press). An activist in the homeless and poor peoples' movements since the mid-eighties, she has participated in many actions and campaigns, working with the San Francisco Union of the Homeless, Food Not Bombs, and the Homeless Task Force, once being taken to court "for feeding the poor without a permit." Menefee currently resides in San Francisco.

Sara Miles is an award-winning poet and journalist who has covered wars and social movements throughout the Third World. Her book of poems *Native Dancer* was published by Curbstone Press in 1985; she was co-translator of Leonel Rugama's *The Earth is a Satellite of the Moon* (Curbstone Press, 1985) and co-editor of the anthology *Ordinary Women*. Her most recent book is *How to Hack a Party Line: The Democrats on Silicon Valley*. She lives in San Francisco.

Victor Montejo is associate professor of Native American Studies at the University of California at Davis. He is a Jakaltek Maya anthropologist active in issues of human rights and indigenous movements. Montejo is the author of *Testimony: Death of a Guatemalan Village, Popol Vuh: The Sacred Book of the Mayas* (a version for young readers); *Q'anil: Man of Lightning; The Bird Who Cleans the World and Other Mayan Fables; Sculpted Stones*; and *Voices from Exile: Violence and Survival in Modern Maya History*.

Leroy V. Quintana is the author of seven books of poetry and twice winner of an American Book Award from the Before Columbus Foundation. He was born in Albuquerque, New Mexico in 1944, and in 1967-68 served in Vietnam where he kept a notebook, which is the source of many of his poems. He attributes his talent for narrative poetry to his grandparents, who raised him, and told him numerous folktales (cuentos) as a child. At present, he is Professor of English at San Diego Mesa College.

Margaret Randall was born in New York City in 1936 and lived in Latin America for many years. She is known in many contexts—as writer, feminist, oral historian, translator, political activist, and teacher. Her numerous publications include *Sandino's Daughters, Risking A Somersault in the Air, This Is About Incest*, and *Memory Says Yes*. She lives in Albuquerque, New Mexico.

Born in El Paso, Texas, in 1954, **Luis J. Rodríguez** grew up in Watts and the East Los Angeles area. In 1989, his first book, *Poems Across the Pavement*, won the Poetry Center Book Award. *The Concrete River* won a PEN West/Josephine Miles Award, and his memoir, *Always Running: La Vida Loca, Gang Days in L.A.* (Curbstone Press, 1993) received the Carl Sandburg Award and the *Chicago Sun Times* Book of the Year Award for Nonfiction. In 1998, he received the Hispanic Heritage Award for

Excellence in Literature. His most recent works are a book of poetry entitled *Trochemoche* and two illustrated children's books: *América Is Her Name* and *It Doesn't Have to Be This Way: A Barrio Story*. At present he is working with peacemakers among gang members in Los Angeles and other parts of the US, as well as providing the editorial direction for Tía Chucha Press, which publishes emerging, socially-conscious poets.

Leonel Rugama (1949-1970) was born in Estelí, Nicaragua. In 1967 he joined the FSLN (Sandinista National Liberation Front). Rugama died, along with three others, fighting Somoza's National Guard in Managua, on January 15, 1970, at the age of 20. *The Earth is a Satellite of the Moon* was published by Curbstone Press in 1987.

Cheryl Savageau's second book of poetry, *Dirt Road Home*, was a finalist for the 1996 Paterson Prize. She has received fellowships in poetry from the National Endowment for the Arts and the Massachusetts Artists Foundation. Her poetry has been widely anthologized. She is also the author of the award-winning children's book, *Muskrat Will Be Swimming*.

Richard Schaaf is the author of one of Curbstone Press's earliest books, *Revolutionary at Home*. He co-translated several books, including Roque Dalton's *Miguel Mármol*. Editor of Azul Editions, a press publishing literature of the Americas, he lives in Washington, DC, with his wife Lise.

James Scully, the founding editor of Curbstone's "Art on the Line" chapbook series, was born in 1937 in New Haven, Connecticut. His book, *Santiago Poems*, written about conditions during Pinochet's dictatorship in Chile, was the first book published by Curbstone Press (1975). His other books of poetry include *Raging Beauty, The Marches, Avenue of the Americas,* and *Apollo Helmet*. His essays, *Line Break: Poetry as Social Practice,* was published in 1988. He lives in San Francisco.

Susan Sherman, poet, playwright, essayist, and editor of IKON magazine, has had twelve plays produced off-off Broadway, and has published four collections of poetry and the translation of a Cuban play by Pepe Carril, *Shango de Ima*. Her most recent awards include a 1997 New York Foundation for the Arts fellowship and a Puffin Foundation grant. She is currently working on a personal chronicle of the Fifties and Sixties. Her collected essays and poems, *The Color of the Heart: Writing from Struggle & Change 1959-1990*, was published by Curbstone Press in 1990.

Edgar Silex is the author of *Through All The Displacements* (Curbstone, 1995) and *Even The Dead Have Memories* (chapbook). A native of El Paso, Texas, he calls upon his Native American, Hispanic, and European heritages in his writing. Silex's poems have been included in *Callaloo, Chants, Chiron Review, The Haight-Ashbury Literary Journal, The Hispanic Culture Review*, and others. He has received fellowships from the National Endowment for the Arts and the Maryland State Arts Council. Mr. Silex teaches at St. Mary's College of Maryland and lives with his family in Laurel, Maryland. His new book, *Wounds of Forgiveness*, is due to be published soon.

William Jay Smith, author of more than fifty books of poetry, translation, and criticism, has had a distinguished publishing career spanning fifty-two years. His poetry publications include *The Cherokee Lottery* (Curbstone Press, 2000), and *The World Beneath the Window: Poems 1937-1997*. Smith has received awards from both the French and Swedish Academies and from the government of Hungary. Two of his ten collections of poetry were finalists for the National Book Award, and he served as Consultant in Poetry to the Library of Congress (the position now called Poet Laureate) from 1968 to 1970. He divides his time between Cummington, Massachusetts, and Paris.

Roberto Sosa was born in Yoro, Honduras, in 1930. Sosa is the editor of *Presente*, serves as president of the Honduran Journalists' Union, and teaches literature at the Universidad Nacional Autónoma de Honduras. Among his works are *Caligrams, Walls, The Sea Inside* (Juan Ramón Molinas Award), *The Poor* (Adonais Award), *A Brief Study of Poetry and Its Creation, A World For All Divided* (Casa de las Américas Award) and *The Common Grief* (published by Curbstone Press in 1994). His poetry has been translated into French, German, Russian and English. He lives in Honduras's capital city, Tegucigalpa.

Alfonso Quijada Urías was born December 8, 1940, in El Salvador. He has spent much of his life in exile, first in Nicaragua, then in Mexico, where he worked as a journalist, and later in Canada. He has published three volumes of poetry and four collections of stories in Spanish. Curbstone published *They Come and Knock on the Door* in a bilingual edition in 1991.

Clemente Soto Vélez (1905-1993) was born in Lares, Puerto Rico. In 1928, Soto Vélez co-founded a literary movement: La Atalaya de los Dioses (The Watchtower of the Gods), which quickly evolved into a major force in Puerto Rico. Soto Vélez was arrested and imprisoned several times for his pro-independence speeches, writings, and activities. In 1942, he settled in New York City, where he exerted a considerable influence on the younger generation of writers. His books include *Escalio, Abrazo interno, Arboles, Caballo de palo*, and *La tierra prometida*. He died in Puerto Rico in 1993, recognized as a major poet. In 1991, Curbstone published *The Blood That Keeps Singing*, selected poems published in a bilingual edition.

Born in 1941, in the small town of San Marcos, Texas, **Tino Villanueva**, a former migrant worker, assembly-line furniture builder, and army supply clerk, teaches at Boston University and is the founder and editor of *Imagine: International Chicano*

Poetry Journal. He has published several volumes of poetry including *Hay Otra Voz Poems*, *Shaking off the Dark*, *Crónica de mis años peores*, published as *Chronicle of My Worst Years*, and *Scene from the Movie GIANT* (Curbstone, 1993) which won an American Book Award.

Poet, painter, and psychologist, **Daisy Zamora** was a combatant in the national Sandinista Liberation Front and served as Vice Minister of Culture after the 1979 revolution. Her first collection of poems, *Sendario*, won Nicaragua's national poetry prize, Mariano Fiallos Gil, in 1977. She has published three books in Spanish, *La violenta espuma*, *En limpio se escribe la vida* and *A cada quién la vida*. Her work available in English translation include *Clean Slate* (Curbstone, 1993) and *Riverbed of Memory*. She is presented in the Bill Moyers "Language of Life" series that first aired on PBS in 1995.

Editor of this anthology:

Martín Espada was born in Brooklyn, New York, in 1957. He is the author of six books of poems, most recently *A Mayan Astronomer in Hell's Kitchen* and *Imagine the Angels of Bread*, which won an American Book Award and was a finalist for the National Book Critics Circle Award. He received the PEN/Revson Fellowship as well as the Paterson Poetry Prize for *Rebellion Is the Circle of a Lover's Hands* (Curbstone Press, 1991), a bilingual edition for which Espada co-translated his poems into Spanish. His book of essays, *Zapata's Disciple*, was the recipient of an Independent Publisher Book Award. A former tenant lawyer, Espada is currently professor of English at the University of Massachusetts.

Poetry Like Bread:
Reading Guide

A COMPANION FOR READERS
by Hugh Blumenfeld

These poems were not written to be studied. They were meant to be read. Or better yet, heard. Whole or in part. Alone or among friends and strangers. Reading and hearing them, you must respond and react. Some may inspire you, knock the wind out of you—make you indignant, sad, joyous, ashamed. Whether you drop this book, seek out others like it, join a social action group, write letters to your elected representatives, or write poems and histories of your own, your reaction will be as political as the poems themselves.

Some of the subjects of these poems may be unfamiliar to you. Many relate stories from war-torn Central and South America, where U.S. policy has had a huge impact on people's lives. Most of the rest are the voices of the voiceless here in the U.S.: Latinos and women, Native Americans and African Americans, Vietnam veterans and Vietnamese, migrant workers and exiles, prison inmates, blue collar workers, the homeless. It's the poet's job to open up and validate these worlds to us, to rouse us from our sleep. Our job, once roused, is to learn. To learn and to act.

So, this essay is not a study guide to help you understand the poems. Its purpose is to help you use the poems to understand the world and yourself as an actor in it. If you've never read much poetry before, *Poetry Like Bread* is a good place to start. If you have read poetry before but never liked or understood it, it's a good place to start over. Here is a chance to reintroduce yourself to poetry, to rediscover your native talent for reading literature and enjoying it.

1. HOW TO READ *POETRY LIKE BREAD*

Poetry is too often taught backwards. Many teachers seem to think that we must know everything they have spent years learning before we can appreciate poems as they do. So we get used to having them direct us to the most "important" poems and even to the most crucial passages. But choosing poems and passages to focus on is the most rewarding part of reading. You don't have to pick out the "best" poems or the most "important" passages— that kind of thinking is also backwards. The "best" and "most important" works are simply those that readers have chosen most often to either enjoy or question over the years. And their judgments change over time. So the question is simply whether you will be an onlooker in this process or an active participant.

All you have to do to read actively is to take notice of the poems and parts of poems *that most affect you*—one way or the other. Read around in the anthology, then pick out the following (remember, no teacher can do this for you; there are no right answers):

- A poem you like or admire (you don't have to know why)
- A poem you find difficult to understand
- A poem that doesn't really seem like a poem
- A poem that disturbs or angers you
- A poem that simply stays in your thoughts

Then, within these poems, start to single out lines you respond to powerfully or find yourself remembering, using the same five criteria. You can even focus on single words that seem powerful to you or whose sound, position, or associations seem to have a special significance.

Then, you can do what writers usually do at this point. They write something in response—whether it is a journal entry or another poem. It might be a piece on the same subject—a result of feeling either sympathetic or provoked. Or, it might be a piece that uses a similar tactic. You might respond to Leo Connellan's "Amelia, Mrs. Brooks of My Old Childhood" by writing a letter to a long-lost friend, or to Naomi Ayala's description of poverty—"a slick / silvery fish between your hands"—by trying to find the right metaphors for a difficult condition of your own. You might experiment with a certain form, like Nguyen Duy's two-line stanzas, which help make "The Morning After the War Ended" so attentive and quiet. And try reading Martín Espada's "La Tumba de Buenaventura Roig" without at least imagining a poem in which each stanza begins with the name of one of your own ancestors. These kinds of responses can teach you more about a poem and how it works than any amount of literary analysis.

You can also try to account for your responses. This is the *only* purpose of what critics call poetic analysis. There are no *right* responses, but by examining them they *evolve,* becoming richer and more complex. So, you might begin by asking yourself:

- Do the poems/lines/words you admire/detest/puzzle over have anything in common? Can you notice any connections at all?
- Can you put your preferences, biases, and questions into words?

This is not easy, and any advice might limit you. Some obvious connections, however, might be that violence and profanity disturb you, or poems about cities attract you. Maybe you are unbalanced by choppy lines or enjoy poems that paint vivid pictures.

Nothing is too simpleminded to be useful. No personal experience or bias is irrelevant. The challenge is to be honest about your biases, your motives, your areas of expertise and ignorance. Sometimes an unusual point of view brings out the most profound meanings in a poem or raises the deepest questions. Your vantage point, with all its limitations, offers a unique way to see the poem. And though your responses will always be valid for *you,* to understand them and have them make sense to others, you have to be conscious of *who you are*:

- Who are you? What experiences define how you think, how you feel?
- What are you? How do race, gender, class, nationality, or religion form your identity and how you see yourself in relation to others?
- What do you know? What are your areas of expertise and ignorance?
- What do you want? What are your hopes and aspirations?

Not knowing Spanish may make some poems seem inaccessible, yet it may also make you feel the presence of the other culture more strongly. Some poems might seem like they'd have more relevance to you if you were poor—on the other hand, they might be less likely to shake you up. So, your viewpoint doesn't necessarily determine your response to a poem, just the path you take.

Difficulties are also easier to solve if you try to identify exactly what it is you "don't understand." What knowledge and experience are you missing that keeps you from fully responding or understanding your response?

• How much of your difficulty involves knowledge about the world? (History, geography, culture, science)
• How much of your difficulty involves knowledge about words? (foreign language, unfamiliar vocabulary, confusing syntax,)
• How much of your difficulty involves knowledge about literature? (allusions to books you haven't read, unfamiliarity with formal conventions)

Once you start to isolate your difficulties, it's easier to overcome them or respond to the poem despite them. Sometimes, just articulating the difficulty as a question is enough: "What countries do James Scully's poems take place in?" One approach to this factual question is to look for clues and narrow down the choices—or go find out. Another approach, though, is to ask why Scully omitted this detail. Are we supposed to know (and so how does not knowing make you feel)? What difference does location make (could it be L.A.? Chile? Either?)?

A more literary question might be: "Is the speaker in Eileen Kostiner's poem "Mastectomy" describing one or just imagining it?" The factual approach is to do research on the author. This might provide an answer or explain the poet's interest in a subject. Another approach is to examine the words and phrases that seem ambiguous to see if they really allow both possibilities. See how your response changes in either case. Which way makes it more interesting to you? Can it suggest both things at the same time? How did she *do* that? Your response and understanding will deepen even if firm answers can't be found.

Reading poetry on your own, you have to use your own instincts about what's beautiful and important. You have to honor the difficulties you face with a sense of curiosity instead of panic. You have to believe that you *are* the reader the poet imagined. Often a poem's primary function is to motivate readers to go out and learn more about the facts and issues behind the immediate, vivid experience it has just delivered. But reading on your own doesn't mean you have to read alone. There is a quality of voice in these poems that imagines being shared, read or recited among friends. Unlike other poems, they seem to demand a social response, whether affirmation or dissent. So, although you can read it in the solitude of your room, try taking this book with you to a café or a park or a public library. Read these poems on a train or bus during rush hour. They go well with a cheap meal or a cup of coffee.

When you can, read them out loud, either to yourself or to friends. They come alive this way. Sharing the poems also gives you the chance to fill in the gaps in your knowledge more naturally and to discuss the issues they raise. You may be surprised to find out how many of the people you know have traveled, have been to prison, have experienced union-busting tactics, or just know a little Spanish. Poems should not exist in a vacuum. They are part of the social fabric, and urge us to make them part of our ongoing dialogue with each other.

A word about the inclusion of Spanish text: it makes the book accessible to Spanish speakers, of course, of which there are 25 million here in the United States, and over 300 million more around the world. But including the Spanish also plays an important role for English speakers. It makes a strong political statement, reminding us that not everyone in the world speaks English, even here at home. So, even if you don't know any Spanish, try reading these pages out loud or to yourself. Imagine living in the world of this language and its sounds (there are also poems in Vietnamese and Italian—go for the texture of the sounds, the movement of your tongue...). You will also be surprised by how much you can pick up by using the facing translations. If you know some Spanish, notice how the book invites you in on a more intimate level.

2. WHAT POEMS ARE REALLY ABOUT

The political nature of this collection may strike you as unusual, but in many ways it reflects the majority of poetry written in the world. A brief glance at almost any traditional folk music or at our own popular music from blues to punk is enough to confirm this. But political themes run through the "classics" as well, from the Bible to Robert Frost. If the poets in *Poetry Like Bread* are unique, it is in the way they combine the directness of folk and popular traditions with the quiet complexity we call literary, creating poems that are socially engaged and addressed to the people whose lives they hope to change.

The most common complaint people make about poetry is: "Why can't poets just say what they mean?" It always seems like they're hiding something on purpose. But the opposite is usually the case. The best poems are tools—instead of telling a truth, they guide us into discovering it for ourselves. Knowing a truth, after all, is less important than discovering it, seeing it suddenly, plain as day. A good truth is not a fact or a concept; it is a recognition, a mental event that has to occur. And a good poem can make us relive this act of recognition every time we read it. That moment of discovery, more than the action being described, is the event the poet means to preserve.

Look again at this short poem by Sarah Menefee:

the blood of Colorado miners
machinegunned down by Rockefeller's cops in 1914
forms abstract impressionist smears on canvasses hung
on the boardroom walls of Chase Manhattan Bank

The poem refers to a specific historical moment, and implies a larger class war, accusing the very rich of murdering the working poor. This may be what the poem is "about," but what makes it a poem rather than a political treatise is that it preserves a different moment too—the shock of being in a bank and suddenly seeing not paint but blood. You don't have to know about Pinkerton raids or unions or even share Menefee's political views to imagine that moment and feel the shock. But depending on your knowledge and political views, your response may vary: surprise, disbelief, confusion, anger.

The poem presents a revolutionary idea, but its higher goal is to create a revolution in consciousness. For one moment, relived with each reading, the poet makes your mind work differently, combining thought, sensation, feeling and intuition. Once you've seen this boardroom art the way the poet sees it, you are forever changed. You can never again walk into a bank without wondering where its wealth came from. Abstract art can never again claim to represent nothing. The poet's metaphor gives you a sixth sense: the ability to perceive or intuit labor history as a distinct quality of the material wealth around you. Suddenly, objects no longer appear neutral, conveniently separated from the people who created them and who paid their true cost.

This revolutionary consciousness—experiencing the world as others experience it, seeing ourselves in new relationships to it, and sensing the potential for change—is at the root of what Martín Espada calls the "political imagination." We must see the world in a new way and imagine a new reality before we can bring about change.

This is a tricky business. If the poet tells us too little, it sounds like she is holding back information. If she tells too much, we will not make the discovery for ourselves. If poets often seem to err on the side of telling too little, it's for two reasons. If you leave a bigger gap, you get a bigger spark. You also leave open the possibility that as readers learn more about the world, they will gain more and more from the poem. Its spark, its ability to surprise, never gets used up. Of course, the poet takes a risk here—a risk that this tool for conveying discovery will not work, that the images may never come together in the mind of some readers in a way that will lead to that sudden sense of understanding. But this risk seems small compared to the other risks of being a poet— remember that many of the poets in this book have endured poverty and scorn, have been jailed, deported, tortured and even killed for what they wrote. The risk of failure when important truths are at stake makes poetry—for both writer and reader—a vital activity and not an academic subject.

Reading poetry takes an act of trust on both sides: the poet must believe in readers' native intelligence and perseverance, and readers must believe that the writer has told enough, but not too much. Promoting the idea that you need a lot of knowledge beforehand in order to appreciate a poem fully short circuits the process of discovery. Reading poems motivates us to learn about the world, not the other way around.

You'll notice that most of the poems are written as if we are already supposed to know what they are talking about—the assassination of

Victor Jara, for instance, in James Scully's "Now Sing," or the "disappeared" men and women in poems by Roberto Sosa, Ernesto Cardenal, and Teresa de Jesús, the revolution in Nicaragua, the civil war in El Salvador, the military dictatorships in Guatemala, Honduras, Haiti. You may feel that the poet must be talking to someone else. But the poet invites you to *imagine* that you know, to pretend for a moment that the places and events are part of your world. In order to feel the anguish, the anger, and also the defiance and joy of the speakers and characters in the poems, you have to try to enter into their experience. As Walt Whitman insisted, "what I assume, you shall assume." Once you have felt and seen unfamiliar things through the unfamiliar workings of someone else's mind, your knowledge will be deeper when it comes.

3. HOW A POEM WORKS

A 30-second TV commercial that costs a million dollars to produce and $50,000 every time it airs leaves nothing to chance. Special "hand" models are brought in for close-ups of hands, lip models for kisses. The exact age, sex, weight and skin coloring of the actors is determined by demographic surveys.

Poets, whatever their motivation, leave even less to chance. Because the poet has only a few words to make an experience leap from the reader's imagination, every detail is carefully chosen, even if their choices are sometimes instinctive and spontaneous rather than conscious and calculated.

Look again at Menefee's tiny poem. It recreates a moment in which the sight of red paint registers as blood, something seemingly out of place in the austere boardroom of a bank. Like a holographic plate, every single fragment of the poem encapsulates the entire image in miniature. The fact that the crimes are hidden, unspeakable, is reflected in the way the murders are only partially alluded to. If you haven't heard of them, that is part of the poet's point. Part of a healthy response is curiosity about the incident. If you don't head for the encyclopedia now, at least your antennae will be primed to pick up pieces of information. And if the information is hard to come by, your concern will only be deepened. Maybe a trip to the encyclopedia is not enough. Maybe what you need is not a poetry course but a course in labor history.

Also, the poet doesn't say "I saw the paintings and they reminded me of the blood that was spilled to pay for them." In the poem, the paint *is* the blood. And notice that the blood comes first. The blood is the reality—it is what the poet sees; the paint is just an illusion. The imagination has turned knowledge into fact.

Though every poem is open to interpretation, the poet's language both evokes and limits the range of responses. Fierce words like "machinegunned," "cops," and "smears" rule out sadness here, even though the deaths of the miners is tragic. In this context, even the word "hung" rings ominously.

Even the line breaks are important here, though the poem has no meter and no rhyme regulating them. The first line, "The blood of Colorado miners" is a single complete image. The blood is not a thought, it is there, existing by itself. The second line is a complete event, the murders. It shocks by itself, even though it is only part of the story. The third line is also a single image, the abstract red designs of the paintings; this allows you to see the paint before trying to understand what it means. The impending doom in the word "hung" is amplified by its position in the line, literally hanging at the end. The last line saves the recognition until the end and delivers the surprise in a single blow.

To the casual observer the poem says "Look again. Don't take anything for granted." To the banker and his allies it says, "We know what you've done. We see." It manages to be an accusation, perhaps even a threat.

Whether you can tell a metaphor from a simile, or an image from a symbol, is not that important. If you let red paint *become* blood instead of just thinking about their similarity, then you have *performed* the metaphor, *created* a mental image. All the poet's tricks are just ways of transforming words from signs with "meanings" attached to them into actual events in your head. Rhythm and rhyme and concrete detail are all ways of giving these mental pictures texture, structure and staying-power. The poem asks that you read at the simplest, most literal level first. *Then, it's the pictures and events that have meaning, not the words.* This is all that is meant by that mysterious term, symbol.

Now, seeing paint as blood is relatively easy. Hearing "a sunflower that sings in its folds" and planting "sensations of sun to become the nightingale that does not sleep" require more magic. These images from Clemente Soto Vélez's poems start to make the division of the senses seem arbitrary. When the brilliance of the sunflower overflows sight, when the sun's heat on your skin sings in the air all night, new senses come into being to capture the intensity of experience. And when Jack Hirshman describes the "tortillas of smog" hanging over Los Angeles, the metaphor does more than just evoke the oily flat layers of polluted air hanging overhead. Tortillas of smog are different from a blanket of smog or even pancakes of smog. The ethnicity of tortillas becomes part of the physical description. The city's Hispanic culture is so dominant that it even shapes the pollution in the air above it. You sense it everywhere.

This is what poetry is best at: creating new experiences, even new senses, through which meanings and emotions are grasped directly, with the sudden force of a spark or explosion. From dreams and nightmares you know that imagined experiences can evoke real responses, and in poetry there is no limit to the experiences you can have.

Let words become things. Let the rhythms of the lines set the tempo for your imagining. What you imagine is a real event in your mind. Trust it. The emotions and thoughts that follow are your particular set of keys. Trust them. Only from these images and responses, sometimes immediately and sometimes only after many years, comes meaning.

IV. EVALUATING WHAT YOU READ

Poetry Like Bread proves that good poetry can be accessible and political without sacrificing artistic integrity. But the book's argument goes further: it reverses the usual standards for judging poems. As the title suggests, poetry *must* be both accessible and engaged in people's everyday political and economic struggles in order to really fulfill its promise and function as art. Poetry is social—not a solitary pursuit of the educated elite—and a complete picture of human experience has to consider not only the individual psyche but our outer, social and political selves which are just as essential to our identity.

The poems go beyond their subject matter and opinions. They also demand engagement from you as you read. They point you outward toward the world. They ask you to consider that who you are "inside" as an individual is shaped by who you are "outside" as a member of a particular gender, class, nationality, and cultural group. And they invite you to break down barriers by making "the other" part of your inner experience.

"Poetry, like bread, is for everyone." It's a sentiment that few students in the United States would find true. Poetry here is more like cake—a sweet luxury—or like caviar, an acquired taste of the well-to-do. Yet, in some areas of the world, poetry still has the nutritional urgency and universality of bread. In the recently liberated countries of Eastern Europe and Latin America, poets have become elected leaders. In countries still under the yoke of oppression, poets are jailed, tortured, and even killed for what they write. When large numbers of people read poetry, learn it by heart and pass it on, it can become dangerous to any government whose power depends on crushing the human spirit. Even a love poem, if it reflects people's dreams and aspirations or evokes a common history, can make a despot uneasy.

The radical content of the poems in *Poetry Like Bread*, and the radical philosophy that allows them to be both beautiful and accessible, make the anthology a perfect way to read poetry without teachers, without specialized knowledge, without accepted cultural values. All you need are the intellectual curiosity to encounter unfamiliar facts and the imaginative curiosity to walk in another's shoes, to experience the world for a little while with different eyes and ears and thoughts. If you are lucky, your reading will strengthen your convictions, or challenge you to rethink and change them. This is poetry; the rest is academic.

*   *   *

HUGH BLUMENFELD is a poet and singer-songwriter who has spent the last six years touring internationally and recording his work. Four collections of his songs, *The Strong In Spirit* (1988), *Barehanded* (1993), *Mozart's Money* (1996) and *Rocket Science* (1998), are available on the independent Prime-CD label in New York. *Big Red* was released in Europe in March 2000 and *Mr Jekyll & Dr Hyde*, an album of topical and satirical songs, is available through his site on the internet (www.hughblumenfeld.com). His songs have appeared on over 20 CD compilations including *The Postcrypt, American Impressionist Songwriters Vol. 2,* and *Fast Folk Musical Magazine*, and have been published in *Sing Out!, Broadside,* and *The Best of Contemporary Folk.*

Mr. Blumenfeld attended M.I.T., the University of Chicago, and N.Y.U., where he received his Ph.D. in Poetics—a short-lived program founded to promote poetry's appeal to a wider audience. After teaching writing, literature and interdisciplinary topics at N.Y.U., Bard College, Brooklyn College, and University of Connecticut, he taught for two years as a professor of English at Eastern Connecticut State University. A former Associate Editor of *Fast Folk* (now part of the Smithsonian collection), Hugh currently edits the substantial Folk Music site at About.com.

CURBSTONE PRESS, INC.

is a non-profit publishing house dedicated to literature that reflects a commitment to social change, with an emphasis on contemporary writing from Latino, Latin American and Vietnamese cultures. Curbstone presents writers who give voice to the unheard in a language that goes beyond denunciation to celebrate, honor and teach. Curbstone builds bridges between its writers and the public – from inner-city to rural areas, colleges to community centers, children to adults. Curbstone seeks out the highest aesthetic expression of the dedication to human rights and intercultural understanding: poetry, testimonies, novels, stories, and children's books.

This mission requires more than just producing books. It requires ensuring that as many people as possible know about these books and read them. To achieve this, a large portion of Curbstone's schedule is dedicated to arranging tours and programs for its authors, working with public school and university teachers to enrich curricula, reaching out to underserved audiences by donating books and conducting readings and community programs, and promoting discussion in the media. It is only through these combined efforts that literature can truly make a difference.

Curbstone Press, like all non-profit presses, depends on the support of individuals, foundations, and government agencies to bring you, the reader, works of literary merit and social significance which might not find a place in profit-driven publishing channels, and to bring the authors and their books into communities across the country. Our sincere thanks to the many individuals who support this endeavor and to the following foundations and government agencies: Connecticut Commission on the Arts, Connecticut Humanities Council, Daphne Seyboldt Culpeper Foundation, J.M. Kaplan Fund, Eric Mathieu King Fund, Lannan Foundation, John D. and Catherine T. MacArthur Foundation, National Endowment for the Arts, Open Society Institute, Puffin Foundation, and the Woodrow Wilson National Fellowship Foundation.

Please support Curbstone's efforts to present the diverse voices and views that make our culture richer. Tax-deductible donations can be made by check or credit card to:
Curbstone Press, 321 Jackson Street, Willimantic, CT 06226
phone: (860) 423-5110   fax: (860) 423-9242
www.curbstone.org